CH

CHAMPIONS

A DIALOGIC APPROACH TO CREATING AN INCLUSIVE CULTURE

FREDERICK A. MILLER, MONICA E. BIGGS, AND JUDITH H. KATZ

BMI Publishing
Bushe-Marshak Institute for Dialogic Organization Development
3898 Trenton Place
North Vancouver, BC
Canada V7R 3G5
info@B-M-Institute.com

Library and Archives Canada Cataloguing in Publication

Title: Change champions: a dialogic approach to creating an inclusive culture/ Frederick A. Miller, Monica E. Biggs, and Judith H. Katz, The Kaleel Jamison Consulting Group, Inc.
Names: Miller, Frederick A., 1946- author. | Biggs, Monica E., 1951- author. | Katz, Judith H., 1950- author.
Description: Series statement: BMI series in dialogic organization development; 8 | Includes bibliographical references.
Identifiers: Canadiana 20220429707 | ISBN 978-1-7771846-5-0 (softcover)
Subjects: LCSH: Diversity in the workplace. | LCSH: Leadership. | LCSH: Organizational change.
Classification: LCC HF5549.5.M5 M55 2022 | DDC 658.3008—dc23

Imprint: BMI Publishing

Page design: Patty Osborne
Illustrations by Brian Tarallo, of Lizard Brain
Graphic design by Kate Hocker

Foreword by the Series Editors

The term Dialogic Organization Development was first used in a 2009 article we published in The Journal of Applied Behavioral Science. In that article, we wanted to describe how we had seen organization development evolve and contrast it with the original form of OD, which we labeled Diagnostic OD. We were unhappy with how OD textbooks continued to treat the newer premises and practices as if they fit the earlier model. We wanted to create a space for people to think about, research, develop, and discuss these newer approaches to change. This book series is a continuation of that ambition and purpose.

Dialogic OD is a still developing mindset (rather than a set of specific methods). It is rooted in two key intellectual movements that are influencing all social science: how social reality is constructed, maintained, and changed by how we talk (post-modernism), and how social systems emerge and self-organize without leadership direction or a plan (complexity science). We have written several articles and book chapters about this, and readers of this book (and all books in the series) are encouraged to access our website, www.b-m-institute.com. Most of our writings and those of some others are available there for free. The articles and book chapters on the website provide a general overview of the theory of Dialogic OD, how it is the same and different from Diagnostic OD, and the basic ideas about leadership, consulting, change, and creating great organizations embedded in Dialogic OD.

Since 2005, we have devoted much of our time and attention to conceptualizing and explaining Dialogic OD. Now we are turning our attention to encouraging presentations of specific dialogic practices applicable to all change methods and approaches. Each of the books in this series is a short, focused, and, most important, practical exploration of one topic intended to continue expanding the theory and practice of Dialogic OD. We hope you enjoy the books. We welcome proposals for further volumes.

If you are relatively new to this set of ideas, you can download and read the free "Companion Booklet to the BMI Series in OD" by visiting www.b-m-institute.com.

—*Gervase R. Bushe & Robert J. Marshak, November, 2022*

Acknowledgments

It takes a village …

Thanks to Paula Robertson, Valerie Davis-Howard, and Melissa Núñez for your recollections and examples of Change Champions in action.

Thanks to David Dart, Placida Gallegos, and especially Kathy Clements for reviewing the manuscript and making it better.

Thanks to Kate Hocker for your work in making the book look so good. Thanks for your artistic touch; you added clarity and beauty. Thanks to Brian Tarallo for your renderings; they brought our words to life. And thanks to Robin Miner-Swartz for your meticulous proofreading; you made the manuscript more readable.

Thanks to Emma Hyland and Analise Agy for shepherding the manuscript through the process to becoming a book and making sure all the parts created a whole.

Thanks to Alison VanDerVolgen and Tara Whittle for once again partnering with us through the process of first idea to adding your brilliance to the final manuscript.

Thanks to our marriage partners, Pauline Kamen Miller, David Biggs, and David Levine, for enduring the hours of time devoted to this book and us not being available to share precious moments with you.

And finally, thanks to Gervase Bushe and Bob Marshak for asking us to include our thinking about creating inclusive cultures that leverage their diversity as a part of their book series. It is an honor and privilege. It is also great to partner with such thought leaders in OD and friends.

Contents

Change Champions are trailblazers—organizational members who volunteer or are invited to go into the unknown to discover and prepare a path for a new reality, a new organization narrative. Like all trailblazers, their role is not an easy one. They will suggest, test, and model new mindsets, language, and behaviors amid the pressures of the prevailing status quo.

Without learning new ways—changing attitudes, values, and behaviors—people cannot make the adaptive leap necessary to thrive in the new environment. The sustainability of change depends on having the people with the problem internalize the change itself.

—*Ronald Heifetz,* Leadership on the Line

They invent the future while dealing with the past.

—*Meg Wheatley,* Finding Our Way

ONE

Introduction

This book explains how using a Dialogic Organization Development (OD) approach with small groups of internal change agents—called Change Champions—accelerates, enhances, and dramatically increases the success of organizational culture change. We describe the path Change Champions take to become effective disruptors of current cultural narratives, the organization's taken-for-granted beliefs, and storylines whose power derives from being so well known and accepted that people would say, "This is just the way things are."

In contrast to organizational change methods that are top-down cascading or large group interventions, Change Champions disperse throughout the organization. We offer examples of how their everyday interactions with peers and leaders change the organizational dialogue to create the opportunity for new narratives about inclusion, leveraging diversity, equity, and access, which transform the culture and support the organization's mission, vision, values, and goals. Our examples and cases are based on actual client situations; however, the names of individuals, organizations, and some details have been disguised.

The Times are Demanding that Organizations Get Different

Joel Barker (1993) famously said that when a paradigm shifts, everything goes back to zero. We would modify that to say everything goes *forward* to zero. In today's state of paradigm-shifting rapid change, there are some knowns, and many unknowns and unknowables. Consider the magnitude of changes impacting our lives now and going forward. Artificial intelligence is anticipating needs and offering solutions that are being taken for granted. The global marketplace is breaking decades-old rules and creating new ones. The rise of social media has changed how people engage with one another and even fight wars. That means that most, if not all, organizations need to change or enhance their culture.

The global COVID-19 pandemic, #MeToo movement, Black Lives Matter, climate change, and other social, political, and environmental movements and lifestyle changes around the globe have pressured many organizations to listen to the voices of their people and the community about causes and issues they care about and to take a public stand. Inside the organization, more people are asking questions about the work they perform. "Why am I doing this?" "How can we do it better?" Many are reconsidering where and when they will work and how they will be treated, choosing to resign or just permanently work from home rather than tolerate colleagues or leaders/managers treating them unfairly or disrespectfully. This has forced organizations to reconsider their hiring and employment practices to attract and retain the talent they need to be competitive.

These massive paradigm shifts have created challenges beyond the ability of a small group of leaders and their "go-to" people to figure out. Instead, organizations must optimize and maximize the contributions of *all* their people. They need to create an organizational culture that is inclusive and equitable, leveraging the full range of people's skills, knowledge, and experience to meet the complexity that today's organizations face. In such a culture, people are freer to voice their opinions, exercise their agency to effect improvements and change, collaborate more fully with others, and, most importantly, willingly give their discretionary energy for the betterment of the organization.

Taking a Dialogic OD Approach

Through our client work at The Kaleel Jamison Consulting Group, Inc. (KJCG) and our learning over the years, we have discovered that it is helpful to position inclusion not as an endpoint but as the means to improve individual, team, and organization performance. We see inclusion as a HOW—how the culture makes it safe for people to bring their different ideas, perspectives, and talents; how teams interact more effectively to drive greater collaboration and innovation; and how an organization aligns its culture with its strategies for higher operational performance.

Taking a dialogic approach to culture change efforts is strongly supported by what we have observed and learned in our 50-plus years of assisting organizations with culture-shaping efforts:

- The bandwidth of behavior the organization and its culture deem acceptable is probably too narrow.
- The organization has probably hired many of the right people but is not enabling them to bring their wisdom and do their best work.
- Many people in the organization are already thinking of solutions to most challenges.
- Engaging and including the organization's people will unleash unrealized potential.
- Significant and sustainable culture change is only possible if everyone in the organization learns to show up differently.

Although our focus is culture change related to inclusion, leveraging diversity, equity, and access, we believe the dialogic processes used in a Change Champion intervention can be applied to other large-scale transformation efforts such as quality, safety, sustainability, and enterprise agility. We hope the reader will explore the possibilities of using a Change Champion-type of intervention in their organization.

A Roadmap to a Dialogic OD Approach to Culture Change

The core change processes in Dialogic OD methods, as proposed by Bushe and Marshak (2014), provide a roadmap to how Change Champions experience and then use their role to:

1. *Disrupt* current core narratives and patterns of interaction in which the mindsets, language, and behaviors impede people from doing their best work.
2. Stimulate the *emergence* of new patterns of interaction, which yield higher organization, team, and individual performance.
3. Uncover and introduce a *generative image* that provides a frame for people to think and act in ways they were afraid to or couldn't before.
4. Propose and unleash *new narratives* about inclusion, leveraging diversity, equity, access, and higher performance that stimulate people to get different.
5. Amplify *new narratives* with success stories about how inclusion,

leveraging diversity, equity, and access accelerate the organization's success in accomplishing its purpose and critical objectives.

6. Continue to *adapt* the new narratives to a changing environment, so the organization constantly looks for opportunities to enhance and transform its culture.

How the Book Is Organized

The chapters are organized to reflect how a Change Champion intervention typically unfolds as a Dialogic OD change strategy. Starting with Chapter Three, an OD practitioner's checklist is provided at the end of each chapter.

In Chapter Two, "The Tale of TechCo," a preview of the Change Champion intervention is presented through the story of an organization that, like many others, is faced with an increasingly uncertain and volatile environment. A cultural transformation is necessary if they want to thrive. Using a Dialogic OD approach, the leaders successfully prepare and deploy the Change Champions process to initiate and accelerate a culture change.

Chapter Three, "Getting the Organization Ready," provides the steps for positioning a Change Champion strategy. This includes identifying and preparing Executive Sponsors and engaging a cross-section of people in group dialogues to discover the current narratives about what life is like in the organization and assess readiness for culture change.

Chapter Four, "Creating the Change Champion Cohort," describes the Change Champion enrollment process, including orienting their managers to the Change Champion's role and eliciting their support. We also explain how to create a safe container where Change Champions can have transformative conversations.

Chapter Five, "Disrupting and Transforming Mindsets," describes several learning activities that disrupt and transform mindsets about differences and introduce new language and inclusive behaviors that help generate new narratives about inclusion, leveraging diversity, equity, access to achieve higher organizational performance.

Chapter Six, "How Change Champions Accelerate Culture Change," focuses on four ways Change Champions accelerate culture change: (a) modeling inclusive mindsets, language, and behaviors in their day-to-day interactions; (b) intervening in conversations and interactions contrary to the new emerging narratives; (c) sharpening the focus of the culture change into an image of where the organization needs to *evolve from* and *move to*; and (d) enrolling groups of allies who partner with Change Champions to spread the new narratives throughout the organization.

Chapter Seven, "Spreading and Embedding the Change," explains how success stories help spread and amplify the change; and how Human Resources must adapt people and management systems to sustain the new culture.

Chapter Eight, "Supporting Change Champions During the Change Process," focuses on supporting Change Champions as they fan out into the organization. It describes how they can respond to several common challenges in their change agent role.

Chapter Nine, "Establishing the Platform for the Future," offers thoughts about the imperative for culture change if organizations wish to thrive in the coming years.

Working Definitions

The conversation regarding inclusion, leveraging diversity, equity, and access, is broad and evolving. Definitions for key terms are presented as a framework for the discussion in this book (Figure 1-1).

Figure 1-1: Definitions

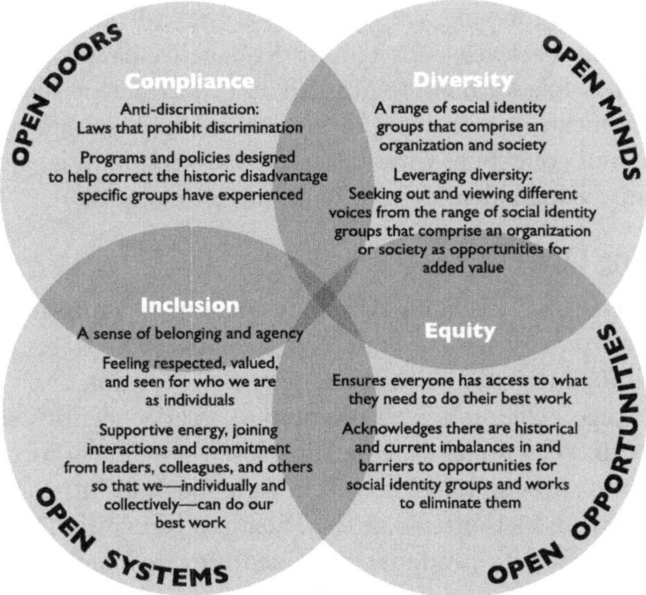

We are intentional in our language and place *inclusion* first when referring to inclusion, leveraging diversity, equity, and access, for several reasons:

- We have experienced inclusion as something most people, if not all, want in the workplace. It becomes something people can support and join.
- The term *diversity* has mixed reactions and can create resistance before people know what it entirely means for a given organization.
- We have found that when positioned effectively, leading with inclusion results in a better understanding of diversity, encouraging people to support their colleagues who bring other dimensions of differences, resulting in increased team and organization knowledge, perspective, and success.

Inclusion

Inclusion is a sense of belonging and agency—feeling a sense of ownership and empowerment to act whenever needed to support the organization's well-being.

Inclusion is feeling respected, valued, and seen for who we are as individuals. There is a level of supportive energy, joining interactions, and commitment from leaders, colleagues, and others so that we—individually and collectively—can do our best work (Katz & Miller, 2010).

Inclusion is a fundamental practice—at the individual, pair, group, and organizational levels—for gaining the benefits that people offer and making it possible for them to flourish and contribute at their best. To experience inclusion, every organizational member should be able to engage in and contribute without feeling the need to hide, give up, or compromise valued identities or qualities (Ferdman, 2010).

Leveraging Diversity

We are diverse just by existing. Diversity encompasses the range of similarities and differences everyone brings to the workplace, including but not limited to national origin, language, race, color, disability, ethnicity, sex, age, religion, sexual orientation, gender identity, socioeconomic status, veteran status, education level, style (such as cognitive, learning, and work styles), interaction style (such as introversion and extraversion), and family structures. There is a recognition that people have multiple identities and that these identities are intersectional. Each identity impacts the other; each has different salience and impact in different contexts and different people. Leveraging diversity means finding opportunities for adding value by seeking out and ensuring the range of social identity groups is heard.

Equity

Equity refers to fairness and justice and is distinguished from equality (Figure 1-2). Whereas equality assumes that all people have access to the same advantages and opportunities, equity acknowledges that we do not all start from the same place, we are not at the same place on our journey, nor do we have the same skills, potential, or aspirations.

Figure 1-2: Equality vs. Equity

Access

Improving access means reducing the organization's economic, social, communication, and physical barriers to resources, information, opportunities, and activities. Creating a more accessible and equitable work environment is an ongoing process of assessing, acknowledging, and removing intentional and unintentional obstacles that arise from assumptions, bias, or systemic structures (National Association of Colleges and Employers, 2021).

Summary

This chapter introduces the Change Champion intervention as a Dialogic OD approach to accelerate organizational culture change. We describe the uncertain and volatile environment in which many organizations find themselves, presenting challenges well beyond the ability of a small group of leaders and their "go-to" people to figure out. Instead, organizations must optimize and maximize the contributions of all their members. This is imperative for creating an inclusive, equitable, and accessible organizational culture that leverages the full range of people's skills, knowledge, and experience to reach and sustain higher organizational performance.

A Dialogic OD approach for culture change is supported by our consulting experience, which has shown that, while an organization's cultural assumptions, beliefs, and narratives may limit people from doing their best work, fully engaging and including people in changing the culture will unleash them and position the organization to better actualize its mission, vision, values, and goals.

TWO

The Tale of TechCo

We operate the same way we have for many years successfully. However, we will be judged by the actions we take or don't take now to position the organization for today and the future. Without transformational change, which includes taking some risks, we will probably not survive and surely not thrive.

—*CEO, TechCo*

When the CEO of TechCo, a well-known and historically successful organization, opened her speech at the quarterly meeting with these words, she surprised some leaders who expected to hear about the roll-out of a new business model and strategy. Instead, a much more significant challenge was presented: to transform into a winning and inclusive culture where people are engaged, feel they belong, and can do their best work. "Unfortunately, smart people with great ideas are not being heard," she said, "at a time when we need them most." She continued, "With greater inclusion, leveraging our diversity, being a more equitable organization, and ensuring everyone has access to do their best work, we will be better positioned to create an innovative and adaptable culture with the interactions and work processes we need to thrive."

Like many organizations, TechCo earned its place as a market leader by focusing on process efficiency and the reliable production of high-quality goods and services. Over time, their standardization of materials and processes had been extended into a machine-like, one-size-fits-all mindset about people management. The result was an organizational culture that rewarded sameness and tended to include, acknowledge, and reward only a narrow band of human behaviors and backgrounds.

The narrow bandwidth also impacted how much difference people could bring. People learned over time to fit in, dress like everyone else, and avoid sharing aspects of their personal culture and experience that might differ from the norm. They kept their heads down and didn't share new ideas that might better serve their customer base—new products and services that could keep TechCo ahead of their competition.

These cultural narratives and frames that supported them may have worked to some degree for the late-twentieth-century workplace. But now, the leaders at TechCo found themselves in an uncertain and rapidly changing reality. They faced what Heifetz and Linsky (2017) call adaptive challenges: problems not amenable to authoritative expertise, single-point solutions, or standard operating procedures. These challenges included adjusting to new marketing channels (web and social), deciding how to invest in and use new technologies, and managing the flow and economic uncertainty in the supply chain. An increasingly complex task environment required each person to "bring their brains to work" to collaborate, solve complex problems as a team, and share decision-making and accountability for results. When people bring their full thinking ability to their work, they also bring their hearts and dreams. Unfortunately, TechCo's current culture did not consistently support these mindsets and behaviors.

TechCo leaders worried that the organization was ill-prepared to attract and retain the needed talent and would lose its competitive edge. Turnover rates among millennials and others were climbing due to its traditional management culture and practices. New team members expected transparency and equity, especially gender equity in benefits, pay, promotion, and career development. And they wanted challenging work and the agency to influence, and sometimes change, things from "day one."

The CEO and some leaders realized that a transformational change was required to manage these adaptive challenges and execute their new business strategy. However, they were uncertain how to begin. They needed more data about what was happening in these times of personal and societal reassessment.

With the support of the Human Resources team, dialogues began with groups in the organization to learn more about the storylines, frames, policies, and practices that hindered people from doing their best work and those which supported people. The dialogues also revealed people's ideas about a future culture that would enable everyone to contribute at a higher level of performance.

After reviewing the themes from the dialogue sessions, the leaders had a better sense of the organization's need and readiness for change and were prepared to decide how to approach the culture change. They believed that having a more inclusive and diverse organization would improve organizational performance. A change strategy focused on inclusion would open up the organization—unleashing people to address issues and opportunities that the leaders were concerned about and building a base of support for other continuous improvement efforts. The VP of Human Resources suggested they talk to a firm of OD practitioners that used a generative process (Bushe, 2020) that engaged the organization's people and encouraged experimentation and adaptation to new mindsets, language, and behaviors. This change process involved preparing internal change agents, called Change Champions, to speed up the time it takes for cultural transformation. After much discussion with the OD practitioners—and initial education for the senior leaders about inclusion, leveraging diversity, equity, and access—they decided to move forward with this approach.

To form the initial Change Champions cohort, the leaders looked for people who were high performing, had influence with and were respected by their peers, and were leaning into change. Several people volunteered for the role; others were referred by Human Resources, senior leaders, union leaders, and managers. A diverse cohort of 35 Change Champions was selected from all functions, levels, geographic locations, and backgrounds.

In a series of dialogic events designed by the OD practitioners, Change Champions uncovered the organizational stories and taken-for-granted frames that constrained people. They leaned into their discomfort to transform mindsets about diversity/differences. Without a change in mindset—beliefs, assumptions, images, or metaphors that powerfully shape how something is interpreted—the Change Champions would continue to see situations the same old way and develop the same responses no matter how much they may rationally or emotionally wish to change (Marshak, 2020).

Back in their work teams, Change Champions modeled more inclusive interactions and took advantage of teachable moments to offer feedback to others. Their actions created an environment where people more easily spoke up, made problems visible, collaborated on solutions, and leveraged their different skills, experience, and backgrounds, leading to higher individual, pair, team, and organization performance. They formed groups of allies that applied inclusive mindsets and behaviors and leveraged diversity in their teams to propagate the culture change more dynamically and with greater speed (Miller & Davis-Howard, 2022).

To support the emergence of new narratives, the Change Champions proposed a set of clear statements of what aspects of the culture TechCo needed to *evolve from*—mindsets, storylines, language, and cultural artifacts that held it back—and what it aspired to *move to.* These initial FROM→TOs were based on what people said they needed to do their best work and what the organization needed to transform and thrive. The FROM→TOs were shared with the organization in a series of dialogues and revised as people offered feedback about how well they reflected the emerging new narratives. For example, a current narrative negatively impacting product quality was "keep problems hidden." The proposed TO state was "make problems visible and solve them at the root cause."

A "Foot in Both Camps"

The Change Champions became the first to model the new culture TechCo desired. However, it wasn't easy. Change Champions navigated several dilemmas as change agents, none of which had simple fixes. Change Champions often thought and acted ahead of others while still part of the system they were trying to change. With a "foot in both camps," they faced various forms of personal challenge and resistance from team members and the organization. Some managers objected to Change Champions questioning current ways of thinking and operating that had made the organization what it is today. Some objected to them taking "time off" from their "real" work to attend an education event or participate in dialogue or planning sessions. Some disliked that Change Champions were interacting closely with senior leaders. A few team members pressured the Change Champions to "stop rocking the boat" and drop their efforts to challenge the status quo. However, with the support of senior leaders, allies, and each other, the Change Champions managed to persevere with their experiments and generate momentum for new ways of interacting and create new narratives throughout the organization.

From "Me" to "We"

As the critical mass for change expanded in TechCo, mindsets, language, stories, and practices counter to a more inclusive, diverse, and higher-performing organization began to lose value and fade. One of the most significant shifts was replacing a siloed mindset of "me" or "you" with "We." These examples from TechCo's sales, manufacturing, and logistics areas typified the shift:

> The Sales department, which focused solely on revenue targets, used to make commitments that Manufacturing could not fill. The two departments now coordinate their activities from contract negotiation to product delivery. They act as one team working to improve time-to-market and customer satisfaction.
>
> In the Logistics department, new team members, primarily Generation Z, asked for more interaction and feedback from their leader. The leader relocated them closer to his office, which offered more informal exchanges and coaching opportunities. This small change positively impacted the retention of these younger team members, who are now speaking up and working together to solve customer problems.

Moving forward, TechCo found it could adapt quickly to continuous change by regularly engaging people through dialogic processes of collective inquiry, testing new ideas and solutions, and scaling up.

Beyond TechCo

The tale of TechCo foreshadows the chapters that follow, which describe in detail how Change Champions engage in a generative change process (Figure 2-1) based on Bushe (2020), in which they engage in dialogue about *what is* and *what could be*; identify the cultural (adaptive) challenges; and generate new narratives and an image and frame for a desired future state that energizes people to experiment with new mindsets, language, and behaviors. What is learned from experimentation is then scaled up and embedded in new narratives and the organization's formal policies, procedures, and norms.

Figure 2-1: Change Champions' Generative Change Process

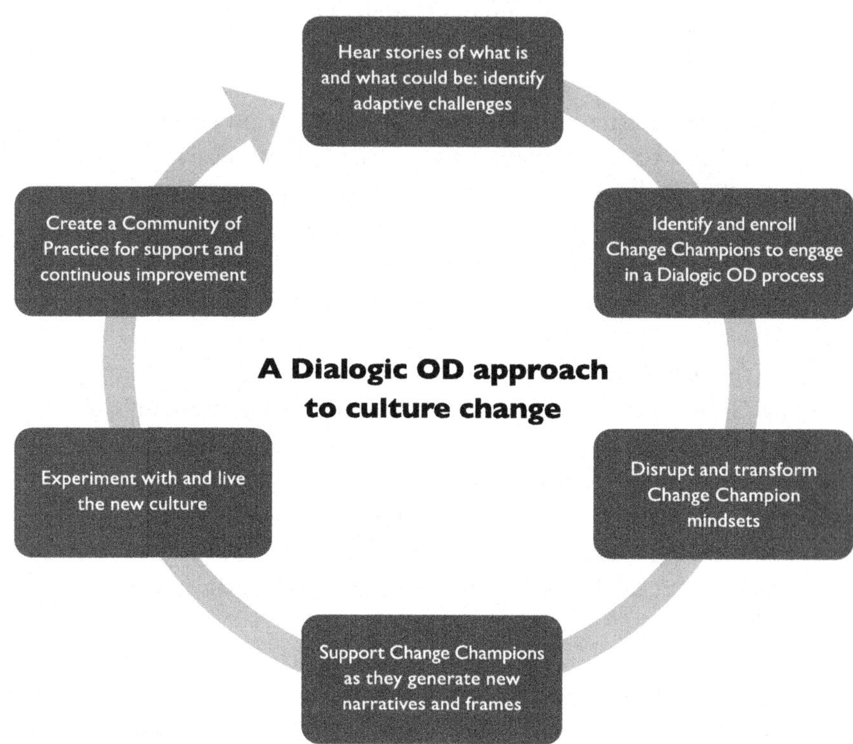

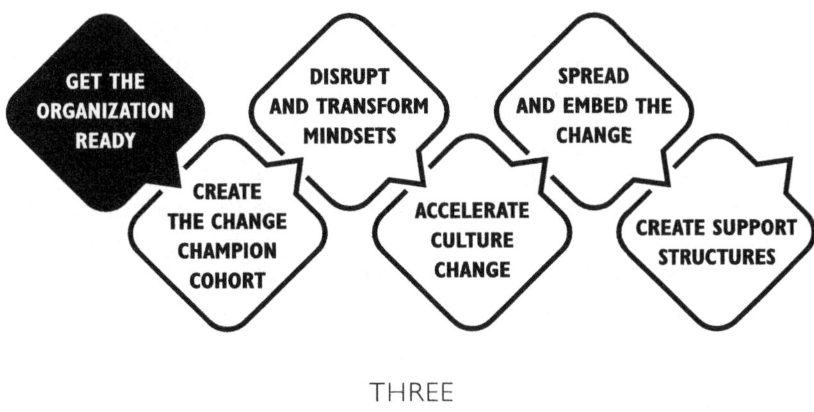

THREE

Getting the Organization Ready

> Major organizational changes create uncertainty. But the point is to move quickly—faster than you are comfortable—because, in hindsight, you will always wish you had made changes even sooner.
>
> —*Irene Rosenfeld, CEO, Mondelez International*

This chapter describes the initial processes for preparing the organization for the Change Champions in their role as disruptors and change agents. These include: (a) preparing senior leaders; (b) identifying Executive Sponsors; and (c) convening a series of organizational dialogues in which people share their stories of life in the organization and ideas for what a new culture could look like.

Preparing Senior Leaders and Identifying Executive Sponsors

The senior leadership team receives initial education to align on the need for the culture change effort and the role of the Change Champions. In the process, the senior leaders—and especially the Executive Sponsors—learn how to be vulnerable and take risks. This helps them model this behavior with the Change Champions, their peers, and the CEO. The education also builds their awareness and ability to practice mindsets and behaviors related to inclusion and leveraging diversity.

Initially, senior leaders are unsure what the change process will involve, what is being asked of them, and what will result. Leading culture change with a Dialogic OD mindset requires a shift from planning and directing to trusting that the right people in the right conversations will "unleash, catalyze, and support the multitude of motivations and ideas among participants in the service of doing the work of the organization and transforming the organization in the desired direction" (Bushe & Storch, 2015, p. 50). They will need to become more comfortable not knowing or having all the answers and let go of their expectation that they can analyze all the variables and figure out the correct answer to the emerging issues (Ellinor & Gerard, 1998).

Gathering Other Perspectives

To help leaders shift their mindsets, we ask them to interview five or six people they select from inside (not direct reports) and outside the organization. The purpose is to gather other perspectives and hear people's ideas, feelings, and hopes related to leadership and workplace culture. We ask them to include several dimensions of difference, such as:

- People in their 20s
- People of color
- White men
- White women
- People new to the organization
- People at various levels
- People outside the organization

Table 3-1 offers several questions leaders use to gather other perspectives.

Table 3-1: Gathering Other Perspectives

• What makes a great leader?
• What are two actions leaders have done and/or need to do to inspire you?

• What do you think is needed to create a workplace where people have the agency to speak up and make decisions about their level of responsibility in the organization?
• What two or three leader behaviors make the most significant difference in your ability to do your best work?
• What are you hearing from your peers about what they think makes an organization a place that attracts and retains talent?
• As you look to the future, what are two things leaders need to be thinking about to create a place where you and your peers would want to work?
• What are two actions you think an organization should take to ensure that talented people can grow, develop, and want to stay?

The senior leaders meet to share what they have heard and learned from their conversations:

- Were there any surprises in what people said?
- Which comments (desires, hopes, concerns) stand out to you as different from your experience in the organization?
- Which comments shifted/changed your thinking about the needs of people in organizations today?
- What do organizations need to do today to keep and develop top talent?
- Given your conversations and listening to what the other leaders took away from their interactions, what are the most significant challenges to shifting the interactions and culture to support a higher-performing organization where all people feel included and able to do their best work?

In listening to people, leaders often experience a disruption to their personal narratives about leadership and what they believe life is like in the organization.

Executive Sponsors

Two senior leaders are selected to be Executive Sponsors for the Change Champions. Because the efforts of the Change Champions challenge the status quo, they find themselves in a challenging and risky spot. To be successful catalysts for change, the Change Champions require the visible support of high-level leaders willing to provide "air cover" and agency that allows them to take more significant risks and operate outside accepted organizational norms. We have found that having at least two high-level sponsors—one who reports directly to the CEO and one who is the next level down and from another part of the organization—builds sufficient initial support and accountability in the process. (The Executive Sponsor who is two levels below the CEO is usually better positioned to hear and understand the day-to-day experiences of the Change Champions.)

Giving Voice Dialogues

While the Executive Sponsors prepare themselves for their role, we convene Giving Voice dialogues with people who share an identity group to talk about their experiences and think together about how the culture needs to evolve. Giving Voice dialogues:

- Help leaders and OD practitioners gauge the level of organizational readiness for change and the degree of openness for Change Champions to challenge the status quo.
- Tap into the unrest and dissatisfaction with the status quo among some people and in some pockets of the organization.
- Begin to disrupt storylines about who needs to be (or doesn't need to be) included and begin to open the possibility for new narratives to emerge.
- Legitimize conversations that challenge the status quo. While many people may have shared their stories previously, their experiences are usually heard as a series of individual experiences rather than a collective narrative that needs to be addressed.
- Generate a buzz about the potential for a new way of being in the organization and elicit the support of people, including potential Change Champions, willing to get different.

Who Participates?

We meet with the Executive Sponsors and other senior leaders to agree on the criteria for participation in the dialogues. We want formal and informal leaders—people considered "thought leaders" and influencers who are good at their job and well-respected. We want a mix of participants who represent various demographic groups (for example: new hires, women, technicians, parents of young children, African Americans, White men, employees under 30 years old, Latino/Latina employees, people who are close to retirement, frontline managers, LGBTQA+, people with disabilities, people with change roles, members of HR, people working outside the country or state of the organization's main office, etc.). While many organization members might be engaged in similar activities, various subgroups may have very different stories about their experiences at work (Wasserman, 2015).

Senior leaders, Human Resources, Employee/Business Resources Groups, union leaders, and department heads provide the names of potential participants. Once the dialogues are underway, we ask participants to suggest names of other team members who would also be good to talk with, and we include them in later groups. The CEO and/or Executive Sponsors issue the invitations, which state the purpose, time, location, and length of the session (two hours).

We try to talk with at least 10 to 15 percent of the organization. In small organizations (fewer than 500 people), we try to include 60 percent or higher. In addition to the Giving Voice dialogues, in most organizations, we host a few in-person and online dialogue groups open to people from any identity group. Table 3-2 shows our typical process for conducting a Giving Voice dialogue.

Table 3-2: Giving Voice Dialogue Process

1. Agree on selection criteria with Executive Sponsors.
2. Select, schedule, and invite participants. Ensure there are no reporting relationships among participants in a group.
3. In a consulting team of two, decide on roles. While one will host the discussion, observe the group, and encourage participation from participants, the other takes notes. (While it is not always possible, having at least one consultant who shares a social identity with the members of the group is often beneficial to establishing trust more rapidly.)

4. Convene the dialogue: • Welcome participants, thank them for their time. • Review the purpose of the dialogue session. • Share two to three ground rules for a productive conversation. • Establish confidentiality and how data will be used. Ask that others in the room keep confidential what they heard from colleagues. • Respond to questions about the process. • Invite introductions: name, role, time in the organization. • Facilitate dialogue guided by questions (see Table 3-3). • Ask for suggestions for additional participants. • Thank you and close. • Provide our contact information in case people want to follow up or share additional information that they did not feel comfortable sharing in the session.
5. After each session, meet as a consulting team and record additional thoughts and observations. • What stories did we hear? What have we heard before? What patterns did we hear or see in people's comments? What is new information? • What did we notice about where the group "got stuck" or had little to say? • What suggestions for additional participants did we get? • Were there any "stars" who impressed us and have potential to be Change Champions?

6. After all the dialogue sessions, meet as a consulting team to make thematic connections and assess the organization's readiness for change.
   - Review all the stories across the sessions. Identify those stories which were heard most frequently.
   - Identify stories that stand out, seem inconsistent with others, or "strike a chord" in the group.
   - Note patterns. What were the prevailing frames, narratives, and stories we heard about people's experiences, thoughts, and feelings about the organization? What are constraints? What are enablers? What was the same? What was different across groups?
   - What seemed to be the emerging new narratives? Where were they happening?
   - Discuss observations about the degree of readiness for change in the organization. Overall, how ready were people to speak up about challenges in the organizational culture? How risky do we think it will be for Change Champions to challenge the status quo?

7. Meet with the CEO, Executive Sponsors, and other senior leaders to discuss:
   - What was said about what limits people from doing their best work and what supports them?
   - Emerging new narratives that could bring momentum to the change effort.
   - Our sense of the organization's readiness for the culture change and the Change Champion intervention.
   - If they think a culture change will enhance the performance of the organization.
   - Names of people who were "stars" and should be considered as Change Champions.

An Invitation to Tell "My Story"

Because the Giving Voice dialogues include a wide representation of social identity groups, the experiences of people who differ from the majority are heard with as much salience as those of the majority or dominant group in the organization. When people—especially those who feel stifled or cautious—are in dialogue with others like themselves, they more easily share what is holding them back and what needs to change to tap more of their potential. Hearing others share similar stories provides support and a recognition that they are not alone. Furthermore, elements of new narratives begin to emerge in these dialogues, as people feel free to express both their frustrations with the current state and excitement about where change is already emerging.

Interaction Safety

For many people, these dialogues may be their first "official" invitation to tell their stories. They must feel safe to speak out about examples of perceived bias, situations in which they felt a lack of inclusion, and their skepticism about the organization changing. Interaction safety (Miller & Katz, 2018) is created by being clear about the purpose of the dialogue and convening groups small enough (generally six to eight) so people will be more comfortable speaking up. Sessions are scheduled so people with reporting relationships are not together. If people do not want to share their perspectives in a group, we arrange to meet with them in a pair or individually to provide greater safety.

We tell participants that the dialogues' themes will be shared with the CEO, Executive Sponsors, and other senior leaders, and eventually with the Change Champions. Our contract with the group is that their specific comments will stay anonymous, i.e., no names will be attached to their comments, so they can feel safe to talk about their experiences.

Framing the Inquiry

The dialogues are framed with several types of inquiry (Table 3-3), beginning with *informative* "What is going on?" then moving to *affirmative* "What is good and should be kept?" and *critical* "What should change?" and, finally, *generative* "What possibilities could be imagined?" and *strategic* "How do we move forward?" (Southern, 2015).

Table 3-3: Questions for Giving Voice Dialogues

• Assume a good friend has been hired by the organization and asks you what it is like to work here. How would you respond?
• What is life like as a member of your social identity group in this organization?
• How able are you to do your best work? What would have to change to make you better able to do your best work?
• Are there people or groups who have a more difficult time doing their best work and interacting with others because of who they are?
• Which group or groups have more influence in setting the rules and cultural norms?
• What aspects of the culture would you like to see changed?
• What aspects of the culture would you like to see preserved and strengthened?
• How would you change how people interact with you so you can do your best work? Why would that be better?
• What, if anything, is holding the organization back from achieving higher levels of individual, team, and organization performance?

Including Marginalized Groups

It is essential to hear all the different voices of the organization; however, gathering a group of people who feel marginalized can be a challenge. In one case, a large professional services firm was particularly interested in the stories of the LGBTQA+ people in the organization but was having difficulty identifying individuals to join a dialogue session. The number of people who are out in the workplace often does not indicate how many individuals from the group are in the organization. Instead, it usually shows how safe LGBTQA+ people feel.

Our client told one gay man about the small group dialogues, and he suggested that the meeting should be held off-site during off-hours for safety purposes so that no one's manager or co-workers would wonder why they were away. The meeting was publicized solely through word of mouth. More than 50 people showed up. Most of the group did not feel safe to be out in the organization, but they eagerly embraced the opportunity to share some of their concerns and discuss issues they faced in the workplace (Miller & Katz, 2002).

Current and Emerging New Narratives

During the Giving Voice dialogues, we listen for thematic stories or narratives and frames that reflect the current culture, those that limit people's inclusion and ability to do their best work, and those that support it. Narratives are taken-for-granted beliefs and ideas whose power derives from being so well known and accepted that people would say, "This is just the way things are" (Swart, 2015). They powerfully influence organizational processes, strategies, and behaviors by providing a frame through which situations are interpreted, thereby affecting the trajectory of events unfolding (Marshak & Heracleous, 2022).

With Dialogic OD, transformational change occurs when current narratives are altered and new ones emerge that support the change people want and the organization needs. We also listen for evidence of new narratives emerging from some individuals, within some groups, and in some parts of the organization. Inevitably, some areas, functions, or groups change a lot faster than the rest of the organization. These "pockets of readiness" can be leveraged as good starting points for experimenting with the new narratives.

Sharing What We Heard

We meet with the CEO, Executive Sponsors, and other senior leaders to share what we heard in the Giving Voice dialogues and think together and align on an initial Change Champion strategy for the next twelve to eighteen months:

- What positive aspects of the culture need to be kept?
- What should change?

- What emerging narratives in "pockets of readiness" could bring momentum to the change effort?
- What possibilities for the future and hopes for how the organization should move forward are people imagining?
- We offer our sense of the organization's readiness for the culture change and when to launch the Change Champion intervention.

Because the senior leaders were involved in the participant selection process, they are ready to hear the feedback from the Giving Voice dialogues as credible. They are more open to others' narratives as valid for them. Also, some senior leaders participated in Giving Voice dialogues themselves and heard about challenges in the culture firsthand. We remind them that being open to what is possible generates excitement rather than defensiveness.

Examples of Core Narratives

The following are examples of core narratives that, through the efforts of Change Champions and others, were subsequently reframed, providing a more inclusive way for people to interpret situations and interact.

Failure Is Not an Option

It made sense that a global specialty materials company had evolved a risk-averse culture. After all, a mistake in a hazardous operation could cause a devastating calamity, loss of life, and material damage. However, the cultural narratives about how people needed to be in the organization went far beyond physical and material safety.

People told stories of a blaming culture. The narratives were, "If something goes wrong, somebody will fall," and, "It's better to wait and see what the leader wants rather than speak up with an idea that might be rejected as too far-reaching or risky." Although customers were pressuring the organization to innovate and come up with new solutions and products, the behavior of most people was to back away from challenges rather than embrace them. A mistake could be career-limiting or, depending on your manager, career-ending. Competitiveness rather than collaboration was reinforced among team members. It was essential to show up as smart in meetings, and the easiest way to prove your worth was to find fault in a team member's comments or presentation.

Carry the Bag

A solid commitment to customer service differentiated a water and hygiene solutions company from its competition for almost a century. The founder was quoted often: "Make the customer's problem your problem" and "Get the job done." Press releases to investors touted the round-the-clock service provided by employees trained to diagnose customer problems, sell products that would solve those problems, and offer additional advice as needed. Getting the job done required a 24/7 commitment to customers.

To become a leader in the organization, you first had to "carry the bag," which meant spending years in the field selling, installing, and repairing customer equipment. This narrative was firmly embedded in the culture as a significant source of pride and success. However, "carry the bag" became a barrier when the company's growth and expansion attracted new and talented people from other organizations who had not spent time in the field as sales and service technicians. For some new people, it was almost impossible to use their skills, experience, and talents on behalf of the organization or influence others since they had not "carried the bag."

Be Like Us

A Black Employee Network (BEN) was formed in the early 1990s in a midsize consumer products company. Through recruitment, advocacy, and career development, BEN had been successful in helping Black employees become more visible and move into executive positions throughout the company's locations. But, at a network celebration for newly promoted Black employees, the congratulatory words of senior leaders, mostly White, were along the lines of, "We're proud to have you join our ranks," "We like your style—it's like you have been here for many years," and "I wish we had more people like you representing us." Although the leaders' words were well-intentioned, the culture had taught Black

> employees that they had to look and act a certain way to succeed in the organization. In their heads, they heard, "To be accepted, you need to be like us, don't be too different, don't be too Black." In other words, people's value still did not extend to their differences. Black employees were still without agency. They were joining "our ranks" and "our We."

Summary

At the beginning of the culture change effort, two actions help position Change Champions for success as disruptors and change agents. First, Executive Sponsors are selected and prepared for their roles. With some initial education, Sponsors begin their journey to understand the cultural narratives that shape people's experiences—for good and bad—and begin to think about how the culture needs to evolve.

Second, Giving Voice dialogues signal the start of the culture change effort, begin to disrupt storylines that are not serving the organization well, help leaders and OD practitioners gauge the level of readiness for change and the Change Champion intervention, and generate buzz about the potential for a new way of being in the organization.

Checklist for Getting the Organization Ready

- ✓ Identify and prepare senior leaders, including Executive Sponsors, to partner in the change effort and sponsor the Change Champions.
- ✓ Convene organization-wide Giving Voice dialogues. Be sure to include members of marginalized groups.
- ✓ Design an inquiry process that shifts people's sense of *what can be*:
    - o Bring people together in new group configurations.
    - o Ask new questions.
- ✓ Track current and emerging new narratives.
- ✓ Share themes with Executive Sponsors and other senior leaders to inform an initial plan for the Change Champions. (Share themes with Change Champions after they are enrolled.)
- ✓ Look for potential candidates to enroll in the Change Champion cohort.

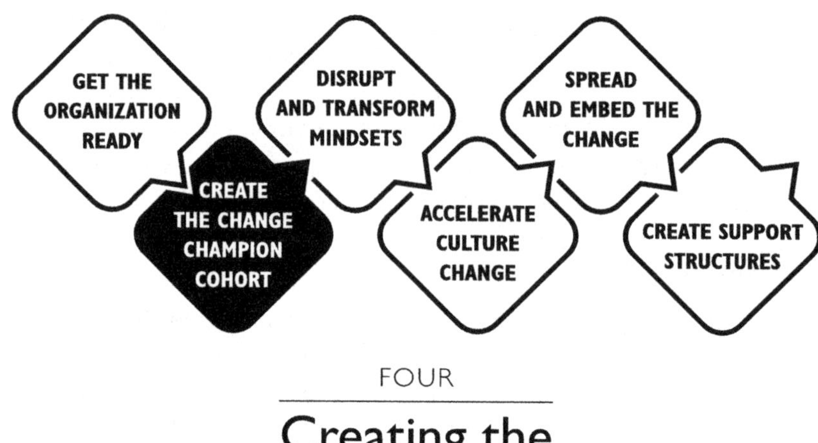

FOUR

Creating the Change Champion Cohort

> Every time you are tempted to react in the same old way, ask if you want to be a prisoner of the past or a pioneer of the future.
>
> —*Deepak Chopra,* The Path to Love: Spiritual Strategies for Healing

The role of Change Champions is not an easy one. Their change-agent work requires courage and the willingness to "break some habits, jump into the mystery, and work with the feedback that comes" (Holman, 2010, p. 114). This chapter outlines the Change Champion enrollment process, what they can expect when their role is fully activated, and how their managers are engaged to support them. We describe how to co-create a safe learning community where Change Champions prepare themselves for their trailblazer role. Finally, we offer how we position ourselves as Dialogic OD practitioners as the cohort develops, beginning as facilitator-trainers and transitioning to hosts.

Enrolling Change Champions

An influential Change Champion cohort consists of thirty to fifty team members from all parts of the organization who have shown the courage to speak up about organizational issues, are respected by their team members, and are forward-thinking about change. They join in a variety of ways: as volunteers, people who are experienced as thought leaders, and people nominated by leaders or their peers[1].

During the Giving Voice dialogues, people participating in these dialogues get excited about the possibility of change, and several submit their names as potential Change Champions. This act of volunteering empowers people and makes a statement that the change effort is gaining momentum, even at this early stage. We also look for people who bravely speak up about changing the culture and suggest to the Executive Sponsors that they be considered for inclusion in the cohort. Some candidates may not be the "usual suspects," i.e., the people usually picked by leadership for special assignments. The "not-usual" suspects bring a voice not always heard in the organization.

The cohort's diversity seeds change, impacts the speed, path, and outcome of self-organizing processes, and supports the emergence of a new narrative that greater inclusion and leveraging of differences is critical to creating a better organization (Eoyang & Holladay, 2013). Although there will be many differences among its members, the goal is to form a cohort whose perspectives are informative about the culture and will enable new narratives to emerge. Once the initial cohort has been identified, we ask, "What areas, functions, or social identity groups in the organization are missing or under-represented? Who else could add perspective and value to the cohort?" These individuals are discussed with the Executive Sponsors and almost always added to the list of potential Change Champions. Table 4-1 offers some additional enrollment dos and don'ts.

1 In a large organization, several Change Champion cohorts are needed to reach the entire organization. The cohorts may be sequential, passing their work and efforts forward to the next cohort, or they could happen in parallel.

Table 4-1: Change Champion Enrollment

DO **Include People Who ...**	**DON'T** **Include People Who ...**
See the added value of new narratives that will result in culture change and are eager to be involved.	Are highly invested in the current narratives; can't see beyond them.
Have their manager's support.	Face a great deal of resistance from their manager.
Are formal or informal leaders; willing to challenge others.	Are unable or unwilling to challenge others.
Are able to manage their workload plus the Change Champion role, even if it's a struggle.	Would jeopardize their job by taking on the additional load of the Change Champion role.
Are willing to "get different."	Fear and resist personal change.

The CEO and/or Executive Sponsors invite potential Change Champions to an orientation session during which we share more about the culture change, expectations of the role, and the education process. The CEO and the Executive Sponsors kick off the meeting by emphasizing the importance of the role of Change Champions to accelerate the culture change process so that individual- and team-level change is visible in six months, pockets of the organization are living the new narratives in six to eighteen months, and within eighteen to twenty-four months, the new culture has taken hold throughout the organization. Then, we explain the selection process, education journey, and time commitment.

We try to give the potential Change Champions all the information and encouragement they need to say "yes!" Potential Change Champions consider if they can fulfill the needs of the role. If so, the CEO and/or Executive Sponsors will ask their manager to support their participation.

Informing and Gaining the Support of Managers

Most Change Champions are reluctant to commit to the role until they are sure their manager/supervisor is informed and supportive. Therefore, a critical factor in encouraging people to join a cohort is the involvement of their managers. The time and energy Change Champions will commit should not be held against them. Instead, their actions should be considered a positive contribution to their team and organization goals and positioning the organization for the future. Managers are invited to a session in which they:

- Learn why change is needed and how everyone will need to shift behaviors for the organization to be even more successful in the future. Like everyone else in the organization, they will need to get different.
- Hear specifics about the requirements of the Change Champion role.
- Ask questions and share any concerns.
- Learn how they will continue to be involved in the Change Champion work, including participation in dialogues and strategy sessions.
- Are introduced to inclusion, leveraging diversity, equity, and access concepts with a short educational lesson.

Managers are asked to agree to the following:

- Enable the Change Champions to attend all education and working sessions.
- Encourage the Change Champions to practice new mindsets, language, and behaviors.
- Visibly support the Change Champions when they experiment with aspects of the new narrative with the manager, team members, and others.
- Experiment with some new mindsets, language, and behaviors as an opportunity to grow as a manager-leader in the organization.
- Show appreciation for the Change Champions' willingness to do this vital work for the organization and recognize their efforts in their performance reviews.

The transparent enrollment process for Change Champions—tapping a group that represents the diversity of organizational voices, giving candidates a choice to join, and engaging leaders and managers in the process—creates energy that starts to spread in the organization, nurturing the hope that maybe *this time* real change will happen.

What Change Champions Will Do

When fully activated, Change Champions model inclusive mindsets, language, and behaviors in all virtual and in-person interactions with team members, leaders, and others. Their role is not to become trainers but to change conversations and interactions. They do this by listening to understand others' perspectives or "street corners," speaking up when team members are not being heard, sharing what they are learning about differences, and demonstrating how including others' ideas, skills, and experiences improves problem-solving, decision-making, and collaboration. By modeling these and other mindsets, language, and behaviors, they create new narratives, providing a frame through which people can interpret situations and interact more inclusively.

How Change Champions engage with others helps change organizational assumptions and generate new meanings about *inclusion* (Who belongs and who has agency? Whose voice is sought out and heard?), *leveraging diversity* (What differences are challenging for the organization to accept and gain from?), *equity* (Who is treated fairly and justly? Who may be denied any organization perks, privilege, opportunities?), and *access* (Who is a full member? Do they have the environment and tools to be successful?).

We describe the development of the Change Champion cohort and their learning journey to becoming change agents in greater detail in the next chapter.

Executive Sponsors Must Enable Agency

Agency is feeling a sense of ownership and empowerment to act whenever needed to support the organization's well-being. The CEO, Executive Sponsors, and the rest of the senior leadership team enable people to take on agency as Change Champions by the following actions:

- Legitimize the work of Change Champions by designating the group by name and publicly sanctioning their activities.
- Communicate why new narratives must be created and then lived

out for the organization to succeed today and tomorrow, and how the efforts of the Change Champions are essential to the organization's ability to create those narratives.

- Ensure that their managers value the Change Champions' participation as part of their formal responsibilities and performance review.
- Ensure that Change Champions have permission to communicate and model new mindsets, language, and behaviors throughout the organization.
- Share learnings from the Change Champions to keep their work visible and a priority and demonstrate support for the change effort.
- Remove barriers to implementing change identified by Change Champions.

The Dialogic OD Practitioner's Role

As Dialogic OD practitioners, we guide the cohort by "being flexible in the moment and adjusting to fit the situation as it is" (McKergow, 2020, p. 23). Our role evolves as the cohort evolves. When the cohort begins the journey, we facilitate activities that teach them about differences, inclusive mindsets and language, and the skills they will need as change agents. These activities serve to disrupt current organizational and personal narratives. We move into the host role as the cohort engages in generative dialogues that transform mindsets and create new narratives about people's inclusion, leveraging diversity, equity, and access in the organization. We resonate with how Roehrig et al. describe it: "The job of the OD practitioner is to create spaces in which useful dialogues can emerge, identify those conversations that are 'juicy' and worth encouraging and find ways to support and keep building on them … to enable the changes in conversations that will affect how the beliefs people have about the future unfold in their interactions with others" (2015, pp. 326–327).

Using Self as Instrument of Change

The Change Champion cohort is supported by a team of three or four OD consultants who will remain with the cohort through their journey. We rely on our experience and skills in large-scale system change, small-group facilitation, and, importantly, our ability to use ourselves as instruments of change. Using self-as-instrument (Cheung-Judge, 2001) depends on reflexively considering our impact—what "meanings we are creating, what narratives our actions privilege and marginalize" (Bushe & Marshak, 2015, p.18)—as well as our ability to make choices to modify that impact. Our mindset is that we are not neutral; we recognize the subjectivity infused in what we say and do and what we don't say and do. Every action we take or don't take can hinder or facilitate the cohort's formation, transformative dialogue, decisions, commitment to the change process, and efforts.

As OD pioneer Edie Seashore advised, we cultivate this awareness by striving to be in tune with the cohort's experience—to be alert and pay attention to what is happening. That involves attending closely to the cohort and being physically, mentally, and emotionally present to see multiple viewpoints. We try to override our discomfort and stay open to alternative interpretations of what is going on and alternative actions available (Minahan & Forrester, 2020).

Focusing on the "Here and Now"

We endeavor to keep our, and the cohort's attention focused on the "here and now"—the actions, events, and feelings occurring in the present time that offer the best opportunities for transformative learning. We have frequent conversations about what we see and feel in the group, which we share with the Change Champions. As the community develops, we notice, name, acknowledge, and appreciate them for behaviors such as:

- Committing to and participating fully in the education sessions and between-session assignments.
- Giving each other grace when someone says something "wrong" and being willing to be—and let others be—imperfect as they learn.
- Demonstrating and accepting expressions of vulnerability: tears, uncertainty, confusion, anger. Staying engaged and curious when others have a different point of view, "I'm not on the same street corner as you! Let's keep talking. Help me understand why you see things that way."
- Demonstrating nonverbal behavior that shows engagement, such as leaning in physically from seats and maintaining respectful eye contact.

- Not interrupting others.
- Gently holding each other accountable to the agreed-upon ground rules.
- Laughing spontaneously and joyfully.
- Experimenting with new behaviors.
- Checking in with each other on breaks; when online, moving to a breakout room to check in with each other.
- Responding with authenticity and directness, even when uncomfortable ("I'm a White guy, and when we get into conversations about race, I'm worried that I'll be blamed for something.").
- Being fully present and minimizing distractions.
- Being aware of one's style and impact on others and asking for feedback ("Am I talking too much?").
- Respectfully challenging leaders ("I would like to offer a different perspective than yours on this topic.").
- Inviting others into the conversation ("We haven't heard much from you. Would you like to join this conversation?").
- Expressing connection and trust.

Co-creating a Learning Community

A learning community is a safe space or container in which dialogues about undiscussables, taboos, and other complex topics related to the focus of the culture change—and how they can lead to higher performance—can happen, disrupting patterns so that new narratives and new ways of interaction can emerge. A learning community is quite different from a typical work environment. At work, Change Champions spend most—if not all—of their time in task groups required to keep the organization productive. They need to be in performing mode: appearing competent and knowledgeable, working out of areas of strength, focusing on correctness, and being error-free. But a different environment—one that invites experimentation and even failure—is needed to shift frames, mindsets, and behaviors. This requires being in a learning mode, or as Kaleel Jamison called it, being "raggedy."

Learning Community Behaviors

A learning community promotes learning as a social, rather than just an individual, act (Watkins & Marsick, 1993). The idea that a diverse group can learn together if all members agree to the same ground rules is powerful. Agreed upon by the Change Champions, these Learning Community Behaviors create parameters and, paradoxically, encourage a free exchange of ideas.

We are reminded of a study conducted several years ago by landscape architect students to discover the effects of a fence around a playground and the consequent impact on preschool children (ASLA 2006 student awards, 2006). The design was simple, and the results were surprising. Teachers took some children to a local playground with no fence; others were taken to a comparable playground with a fence defining its border. Contrary to what many expected, the children in the playground with no fence remained huddled around their teacher, fearful of the dangers if they wandered too far away. Children felt free to explore from one end to the other in the fenced-in playground. In other words, the perimeter fence provided a sense of safety. Likewise, groups engaged in dialogue and learning find it easier to experiment and explore ideas when the boundaries and ground rules are clear and agreed to.

Table 4-2 lists some Learning Community Behaviors (Jensen & Miller, 1995, 1997, 2022) we find helpful in creating the container, enabling the Change Champions to build a foundation for dialogue and transformative conversations. Every group adds to or modifies this list to meet their own needs for safety and learning.

Table 4-2: Learning Community Behaviors

• Give and create interaction safety. Make it safe for yourself and others to take risks, experiment with new behaviors, make mistakes, grow, and change.
• Be self-responsible and self-challenging. Challenge yourself to raise the issues, concerns, worries, and fears important to your learning and the community's efforts.
• Offer grace when you and others make mistakes.
• Listen as an ally and respond. First, listen to and appreciate what others are saying, and take time to fully understand their words and intent. Then, respond with your understanding of what they have said, share how your thoughts connect to theirs.
• Lean into discomfort. See discomfort as an opportunity to learn something new, not something to avoid.
• Experiment with new behaviors to expand your range of responses. You will gain new perspectives as well as increase your skills.
• Accept working through conflict to its resolution as a catalyst for learning.
• Be direct. Don't beat around the bush, sugarcoat, or disassemble for fear of causing hurt or conflict. Give the other person credit for being able to handle your honest feelings or observations.
• Recognize that others may have a different perception or "street corner" from you. Be curious and accept their perspective as valid for them.
• Honor confidentiality. As others share their perceptions, experiences, and feelings, it is important to treat that sharing as a precious gift. Honor their confidence in you by not sharing their confidences with others. Do share your learnings and what is happening with the culture change effort.

Some guidelines are more applicable, depending on the organization and group context. For instance, in a fast-paced sales organization,

Change Champions were direct in their language but needed to slow down to listen before responding. In another organization, where being "nice" meant avoiding disagreement, the Change Champions needed to challenge themselves and others to lean into their discomfort and be willing to raise issues.

We want an environment that supports the interaction safety and stability of the learning community and cultivates conditions for dialogue and the emergence of new narratives. In addition to the Learning Community Behaviors, some things we have found make a real difference are described in the following sections.

Organizing the Physical Space to Encourage Dialogue

Chairs arranged in a circle create an energetic and egalitarian space that encourages attentive listening and intentional speaking, where the Change Champions can lean into discomfort to find their learning edges. Christina Baldwin and Ann Linnea (2010) describe the dynamic created by the circle configuration. "There is a physical and energetic vulnerability to sitting in a circle. We are facing each other, usually without even a table between us. Our soft bellies are exposed, our expressions convey emotional nuance, and our body language is fully visible. Our personal energies begin to link up and overlap and influence each other so that even before the first words are spoken, before the bell rings, and before the host starts check-in, we have taken in a lot of information about who we are" (p. 109).

Depending on the group's needs, we reorganize the room as the session progresses. For example, we might move the chairs into close concentric circles when the group is grappling with a weighty issue and needs to reinforce a sense of safety in the room. Like the Quaker dialogue model, this configuration invites everyone in the room to participate. The Change Champions listen and then ask a question or express a feeling or thought, consciously addressing the whole group rather than an individual. At other times when sharing a concept, we might move to a theater-style set up with chairs in rows to make it easier for participants to see, hear, and focus on the material being presented.

Standing to be Fully Seen and Heard

It is essential that Change Champions feel they belong to a cohort that fully values their difference and voice. This is critical for learning and often becomes a value needed in the new culture. One action that facilitates hearing someone's voice without interruption is asking people to physically stand if they can. Initially, some may protest, "I don't have to stand; people can hear me." However, standing up increases the speaker's ability to be seen and fully heard without interruption. When individuals pause to breathe or think, they don't lose their turn. And, if their most important thought is at the end of their comment, they don't get cut off.

Saying Hello

All sessions, in-person or online, begin with hellos. Connecting via hellos is an invitation to join the conversation and make one's voice heard. The message is, "I see you, and you have value; you belong." This simple action starts the Change Champions on their journey of connecting and establishing trust with other members. It makes it easier for many to speak later since they have already connected with people through the hellos.

We encourage the Change Champions to say an individual hello to each person in the room or virtually join the meeting early so they can say hello to others. It may be surprising, but this small gesture disrupts the norm in many organizations. People head to their workstations instead of saying hello to others or greeting only those they know well. In a virtual workspace, they go straight to the task without any check-in. In many organizations, new or different people get the fewest hellos. Hellos don't show up on the bottom line, so they often get ignored, but when they get ignored for too long, the bottom line suffers (Miller & Katz, 2005). Two Change Champions describe the results when they brought the practice of saying hello to their teams:

> We always say time is money. But what is the cost when people feel left out and invisible? This week, I started saying hello and asked everyone to greet each other at the start of my meeting. It only took a couple of minutes. Energy went up, and people were more eager to speak and offer their ideas.

> Project team members did not turn on their video cameras in online video meetings. We needed to make critical decisions, but we couldn't see each other's faces! I said hello to each person as they became visible and asked everyone to put their video on. They grumbled at first, but it made a big

difference in the willingness of people to participate, connect with each other and take ownership of our collective decisions.

Experimentation is vital to change. Saying hello and seeing someone can start the process of experimenting with new behaviors, which is critical if new narratives are going to be created and adopted.

Introductions

Introductions serve three purposes. First, a norm of listening and fully attending to the speaker is established. While the individual speaks, no one can interrupt. There is full participation—each person takes the floor. Second, the process of disclosure builds collective trust. People allow themselves to be vulnerable. The third purpose of the introductions is to support the continued differentiation among cohort members. The tension of differences provides the potential for emergence, self-organizing, and change, demonstrating the power of diversity. In the large group, each individual responds to questions, including:

- What is the story of your name?
- Where were you born?
- Why did you say yes to becoming a Change Champion?
- What will be the most challenging part of culture change here?

People continue their self-disclosure in several rounds, moving from pairs, then combining into small groups of four, eight, and sixteen. The gradual increase in the size of the groups helps build collective trust as the cohort forms.

Round 1 (in pairs): Where did your ancestors come from? What is one thing you bring to a group that you value?

Round 2 (pairs join to form groups of four): What are two group identities (Figure 4-1) important to you? If you could have a do-over for one event or phase of your life, what would that be?

Round 3 (groups of four join to form groups of eight): What is one thing that is exciting you these days? What is one question you still have about being a Change Champion?

Round 4 (groups of eight join to form groups of sixteen): What will be the most challenging part of changing the culture here? The easiest part?

We reconvene the whole group so people can share their reactions to the process, ask questions about the Change Champion role, and discuss what they see as the most challenging and easiest parts of the culture change process.

Figure 4-1: Group-level Differences that Make a Difference[2]

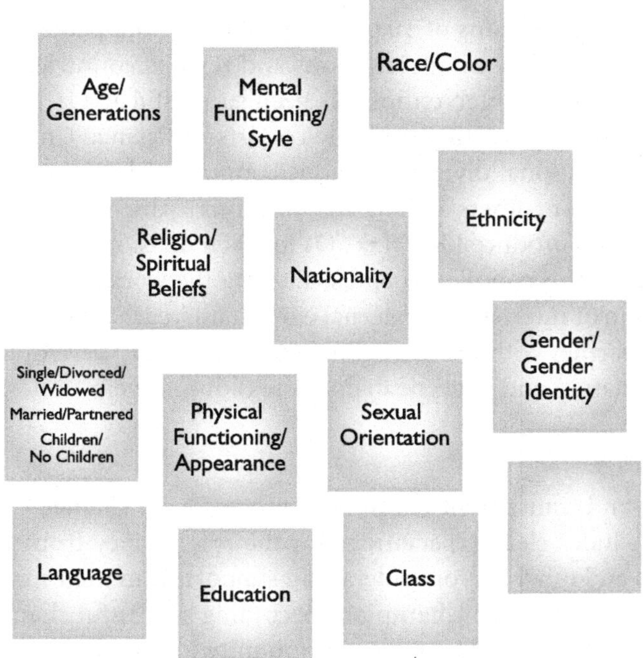

Creating a Learning Community with a Hybrid Cohort

In many organizations, Change Champion cohorts are in a hybrid configuration, with some people physically present together and others present in a virtual online space. Breakout rooms, chat box messaging, and shared applications for recording group work (such as Google Docs) help people connect and be fully included in the learning activities. We adapt the schedule to accommodate cohort members in various time zones and manage "Zoom fatigue" by offering shorter sessions with frequent breaks. (See Stirling-Wilkie (2021) for more advice on hosting online group events.) However, a few sessions, such as those

2 The box with an open space gives people an opportunity to add a group identity not indicated elsewhere, e.g., Veteran status, trauma survivor, Alcoholic Anonymous.

focusing on differences and the "isms," are almost always in person to better assure interaction safety.

A Note about Scale

In this book, we describe a dialogic approach to using Change Champions from the perspective of a cohort of thirty to fifty who shift the organizational narratives in a single organization. Some of our clients are global organizations of 10,000 to 50,000 or more people operating in multiple functional units/divisions and regions/countries/sites. The Change Champion intervention has been successful at a large scale and across cultures by creating multiple cohorts of Change Champions in many organizational divisions/regions/countries. These cohorts gather perspectives from others in their organizations to discover the prevailing narratives and produce FROM→TOs for each division/region/country.

Managing this complexity and sustaining the work globally requires a large team of internal and external consultants, each with a local focus, who can partner with Executive Sponsors on strategy development and implementation and convene dialogue sessions in their locales.

Summary

An open and transparent enrollment process for a Change Champion cohort includes clear expectations for the role, agency from Executive Sponsors and other senior leaders, and support from their managers. A prerequisite to Change Champions becoming successful change agents and role models is a safe learning community to experience disruption, manage the feelings disruption can produce, and self-organize.

As Dialogic OD practitioners, our role as facilitators and hosts is to co-create an inclusive and safe container to encourage generative conversations that will transform the Change Champions' mindsets about differences—an environment where they can experiment with new perspectives, language, and behaviors. We begin the process by purposefully arranging the physical space, setting boundaries with ground rules, saying hello, and building trust with introductions.

Checklist for Creating the Change Champion Cohort

✓ Enroll a diverse cohort of people willing to become Change Champions.

- ✓ Before finalizing the cohort membership, ask them and the Executive Sponsors who is missing to continue to enhance the diversity of the group.
- ✓ Gain agreement on how the Executive Sponsors will create agency for the Change Champions to disrupt the organization.
- ✓ Orient managers and supervisors to the Change Champion role and the expected time commitment. Contract for their support and participation in the education and change process.
- ✓ Co-create a safe learning community by organizing the physical space to encourage dialogue, offering ground rules, inviting people to say hello, and spending time on introductions.
- ✓ Develop multiple cohorts of Change Champions when size requires you to expand the reach across regional locations and cultures.

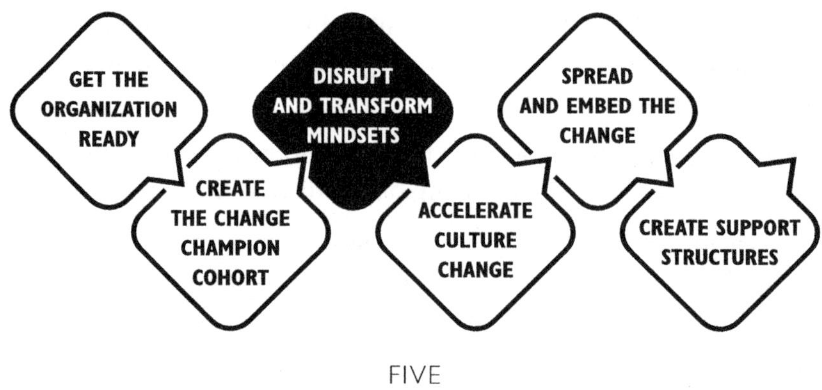

FIVE

Disrupting and Transforming Mindsets

> You can't change anything without causing some degree of disruption. It's impossible; that is exactly what change is. Some people are uncomfortable with the disruption that change causes, but the disruption is necessary if anything is going to change.
>
> —*Afeni Shakur, American civil rights activist*

Before Change Champions begin the work of transforming the organization, they must go through a transformation themselves, personally and as a cohort. In four three-to-four-day sessions (Figure 5-1), we engage the Change Champions in activities and dialogues that help them become more aware of, and then disrupt, the narratives and patterns of interaction constraining people in the organization. Disrupting the current narratives supports the emergence of generative images and new narratives of inclusion, leveraging diversity, equity, and access which take hold first within the cohort and, as described in subsequent chapters, throughout the organization.

Figure 5-1: Change Champion Learning Architecture

SESSION 1	SESSION 2	SESSION 3	SESSION 4
Onboarding and positioning the cohort	**Transforming mindsets and disrupting current narratives**	**Engaging the organization through dialogue**	**Measuring and positioning for ongoing enhancements to the narrative**
Understand why culture change is needed	Dialogue about differences	Create FROM → TO vision statements	Measure progress with success stories and pings (short surveys)
Understand the Change Champion role	Disrupt current narratives	Create new narratives by hosting dialogues throughout the organization	Join Communities of Practice
Co-create a safe learning community	Learn and experiment with new mindsets, language, and behaviors	Accelerate the change with groups of allies (Pods)	Celebrate the completion of this phase of the process
		Expand the narratives by engaging managers and Pod members	Ongoing dialogue sessions and continuous improvement

Probing the Paradox of Differences

Diversity, or difference, is not confined to a particular racial, ethnic, or gender group. Many differences exist even among people who look, sound, and act alike—even "identical" twins are different from each other. On the other hand, all humans have many things in common. One way to frame this natural tension is as a paradox with three levels (Kluckholn, 1955), all true at the same time:

- We are like *all* people. As human beings, we share universal needs (oxygen, food, water, shelter) and want to love and be loved.
- We are like *some* people. We share culture and experience with some others. Our group memberships play a significant role in determining our experience in society and organizations.
- We are like *no other* people. We have a unique thumbprint, genetic code, and collection of preferences, experiences, and aspirations.

Organizations can underestimate the challenges of the change effort if they do not understand and appreciate the complexity of this paradox. Both differences and sameness contribute to organizational effectiveness. Without the "sameness" of a collective purpose, agreed-upon goals, and behavioral norms, differences can potentially pull an organization apart, with different people and groups working against or at odds with each other. Without differences, there is a greater chance that the range of perspectives, information, approaches, and competencies needed for the most effective problem exploration and solving will be absent. But a singular emphasis on sameness makes an organization rigid and inert. The balance between the opposing forces of diversity/differences and sameness keeps an organization positioned to adjust to environmental changes and better see around the next corner. With increased dialogue and engagement, an organization can leverage diverse perspectives while simultaneously emphasizing a shared purpose, values, and goals (Ferdman, 2017; Waldman & Sparr, 2022).

Exploring the Paradox of Differences

Over the course of their education, the Change Champions have many opportunities to explore the paradox of differences. Here is one example.

> The first day focused on introductions of a deeper and more authentic nature than most in the room had ever experienced. The introductions moved many people in the cohort. During an afternoon break in Session One, a Change Champion whose name tag said "John" approached one of the OD consultants. John said he wanted to be brave and honest and asked if he could share his identity as his authentic self, "Joanne."
>
> The following day, when the person some had known and many had seen for ten years as a *man named John* entered the room as a woman named Joanne, the Change Champions expressed a wide range of initial emotions: worry, confusion, curiosity, and full acceptance.
>
> We took steps to ensure interaction safety was present, reminding them of their ground rules with emphasis on honoring confidentiality, leaning into discomfort to learn, and taking responsibility for creating safety for themselves and others. We asked, "Does everyone understand and agree to

these? If so, show thumbs up. If you have a question, show thumbs sideways." We moved on when, after dialogue, everyone in the room had thumbs up and Joanne felt safe enough to fully join the process. She did not want to be outed to the whole organization, so confidentiality was important.

Joanne shared her ongoing exploration of her gender identity, an arduous journey she had been on for many years. She was responsive to the group's awkward and somewhat intrusive questions and comments and was encouraged to draw the line and stop the conversation whenever she liked. Joanne was tearful at several points, saying she felt relieved and anxious. After she finished, people thanked her, gave some supportive hugs, and continued with other members' introductions.

Later, the cohort talked about what they had learned from people sharing who they are and how they feel about aspects of their lives. Their dialogue was guided by questions such as, "What was an 'a-ha' moment from the experience?" "What assumptions do I make about people different from me?" "How do I want to show up with my peers? My manager? This cohort? My family?" "What might it take for me to be my most authentic self in this cohort? In my life?" The dialogue became an initial step on their journey of exploring individual and group differences and challenging personal and organizational assumptions, frames, and biases.

After a couple of months, Joanne felt supported enough by the Change Champions, the Executive Sponsors, and the new narrative about valuing differences to come out to the organization. She assumed a leadership role in forming the organization's first LGBTQA+ network group, offering encouragement and assistance to many who had not felt safe enough to be their authentic selves at work.

Holman (2010) suggests a flow for the emergence of new organizational patterns: a disruption breaks apart the status quo; the system differentiates, surfacing innovations and distinctions among its parts; and, as different elements interact, a new coherence arises. This disruption led the cohort to engage in the inherent messiness of dialogue, which involves "difference, conflict, fantasy, and emotion" (Stacey, 1996, p. 13).

Although it created discomfort for many, the disruption was a gift.

The Change Champions learned to engage around a difference with which many had little exposure or comfort without the fear of being shamed or saying the wrong thing. A new narrative about differences began to emerge—i.e., that talking about differences respectfully and meaningfully can unleash people's energy and open more possibilities for them as individuals, the cohort, and the organization.

Individual Stories of Difference

As OD practitioners, we always work toward system change. Many individuals and organizations need to move from "me" and "you" to a collective "We." But, as Roehrig et al. point out, "Amplifying change in the organization as a whole involves amplifying change in individuals" (2015, p. 327). The Change Champions begin with an exploration of differences at the individual level. Every individual has their own story about how they came to be the person we see today. People sharing who they are and how they feel about aspects of their lives in their introductions and activities, such as Journey of Our Differences (described in the next section), serve to validate individuals. Once individuals feel validated and seen for who they are, they are more willing to give grace to others and their discretionary energy to the organization. We count on this from Change Champions, and the organization needs it from everyone to achieve higher and higher performance.

Journey of Our Differences

We invite each Change Champion to draw a picture in response to a series of questions about their journey to becoming aware of themselves and their differences (Table 5-1). As they create their drawings, they get in touch with the messages they received from family, friends, schools, religious institutions, media, and workplaces that shaped their mindsets and behavior patterns related to differences.

Table 5-1: Questions for Journey of Our Differences

• When growing up, which differences were the most significant in your life?
• When growing up, who were the "strangers" to watch out for, who represented danger?

• When did you realize you were different?
• When did you realize that your group was not in the majority?
• What were the messages from your family, peers, religious and educational institutions, the media, etc., about different groups? Which groups were you taught to avoid and fear?
• What three to five identity groups do you identify with? When did you become aware of your membership in these groups?
• When growing up, which two to three identity groups had the most privilege?
• Which aspects of yourself do you feel valued for at work? Outside of work?
• In which identity groups do you have friends different from you? In which do you not?
• Where are you today in your journey to understand and embrace differences? Which differences do you need to learn more about or be more comfortable with to be a better work partner with people who might have represented/currently represent that difference in the workplace? How will you do that? Who will assist you?

The Change Champions share their drawings in groups of three or four. People choose what they share, and others listen attentively. Some talk about painful experiences of hiding, suppressing differences, or being excluded. Some say they feel ashamed or embarrassed about the messages from parents, teachers, other authority figures, and the media that generate fear of the "other." We encourage everyone to suspend judgment and listen to each other's stories as allies, without interrupting, only asking questions for clarity. These excerpts represent some Change Champions' comments:

> Everything changed when I got to high school. Suddenly, it wasn't OK for me to hang out as a White with my Latino friends from the neighborhood. Even the teachers seemed to reinforce the message that I should stay with my own kind.

My father died when I was a teenager. I had to find a job to help support the family. I found out what it was like to be poor. I was not included in the social life at school because I had to work.

My mom taught me how to talk "White" and act as a cultural White. I did it to survive as a biracial man in school and at work. But it has hurt me with some Blacks.

I never really felt different. But now, I feel increasingly undervalued and overlooked at work because I have a condition that makes walking difficult.
When I came out as a lesbian at school, it was upsetting to have girls leave the locker room when I entered.

My parents used the "N" word. I was embarrassed as a kid, but I admit I absorbed that the color of someone's skin mattered, and Whites were on top.

I grew up in a strict religious household. We didn't mix with people outside our religion. I still have a hard time not being judgmental about people who believe differently than how I was raised.

After everyone shares their pictures, we ask them to reflect on which mindsets may need to change so that they can better value their own and other people's differences to improve their partnerships, teams, and the organization. The cohort reconvenes to offer what they learned from the activity and some examples of mindsets they may need to shift.

Group-level Differences That Make a Difference

The Change Champions continue to probe the paradox of differences, moving from individual to group level. The aspects of ourselves, like *some* people, constitute our connection to specific identity groups, those with whom we share similarities. Many move toward people like themselves when entering a room, group, or organization. If people are not intentional, they stop there.

Depending on the social context, people tend to feel a solid affinity for some of their group identities and not as much for others. For example, in one organization, many identified primarily with their job classification, i.e., whether they were salaried or union. Others identified strongly with their ethnicity, especially those who had immigrated to the United States or were first-generation United States residents and/or had English as a second language. Some said being veterans or parents mattered most. However, a person's group identity can mean more to others than to themselves. For instance, a man in the group identified himself primarily as a Ph.D. rather than a Muslim, but others saw him the opposite way.

We ask the Change Champions to consider which of their identity groups are one-up (i.e., the group treated as privileged, preferred, or favored) in society and which social group identities are one-down. It is worth noting that 95 percent of people in organizations have both one-up identity groups and one-downs. An individual is rarely one-up in all the categories.

An example that people can easily relate to is right- and left-handedness. Most of the tools, procedures, and almost all vehicles are designed to be used by right-handed people. Left-handed people must put up with struggles/adjustments that right-handed people don't need to think about: the swipe and pen on a credit card machine, the number pad on a computer keyboard, scissors, and the flap covering a pant zipper are all designed with the right-handed in mind. Historically, various religious and cultural beliefs associated left-handedness with negative connotations and traits, which are still reflected in left-handed bias in language. The Italians say "mancino" for left-handed, which can also mean "deceitful." The French word for left is "gauche," which in English is translated as "unsophisticated" or "socially awkward."

Group Perception Exchange

In many organizations, what is considered "normal" is a relatively narrow range of styles, views, and ways of interacting. Anything outside the norm is ignored, minimized, or forced to assimilate, discouraging the expression of and undervaluing differences. The Change Champions explore how this dynamic operates at their organization's group and system levels as they engage in the Perception Exchange activity.

For this exercise, we divide the cohort into social identity groups. Each person joins a group that matches one of their social identities. Depending on its makeup, the groups might include Latino/Latinas, White women, people under 30 years old, parents, African American/

Blacks, people with two years or fewer in the organization, union members, White men, and people from parts of the organization located in a different country than headquarters. The task is to draw a group picture based on their collective narratives and perspectives about the organization from the standpoint of that identity group, using the following questions (Table 5-2) as prompts:

Table 5-2: Questions for Perception Exchange

• What is the overall tone/feel of the organization?
• How are people at different organizational levels and areas treated?
• What aspects of the organizational culture today need to be carried into the future?
• What are some aspects that should not be taken into the future?
• Which social identity group is most included in the organization? Which is least included? (Consider the social identity groups we have formed for this activity and all others in the Change Champion cohort.)
• How included are members of your social identity group in the organization on a scale of 0 (low) to 10 (high)?
• What would help your social identity group move closer to a 10?
• What skills, resources, or strengths does your social identity group bring to the organization?
• How would a more inclusive, diverse, equitable, and accessible culture impact organizational success, i.e., accomplishing its mission, vision, and goals?

Here is an example of how this process unfolded in one organization:

> Although the cohort had spent a few days exploring differences, they found the process of separating into these groups unsettling. The White women's group expressed their discomfort that racial and gender divisions are now

being emphasized in the room. This wasn't a theoretical or generalized societal view of group difference; they were seeing and trying to manage their anxiety about uncovering the status and privilege that was or was not afforded these groups in their organization today. After being heard, the White women decided to lean into their discomfort and begin their task.

As people talked and collectively drew images in response to the questions, their focus evolved from a collection of personal views of organization reality to a picture of shared meaning. Talking together about what they saw from their group lens/street corner was fortifying; making art together energized and surprised them.

The under-30 group felt the power of connecting to the "collective field" (Ellinor & Gerard, 1998, p. 248). Their picture vividly showed what limited them and what they wanted to contribute. As one of them said, "We come from different areas in the organization and have never talked together. If you look at our picture, you can see we are on the same wavelength about many things: what we like about the organization, what we think needs to change, and what makes us feel overlooked and patronized. It sucks to have new ideas and not be listened to. Even here in this cohort, we have heard comments like, 'You might not understand,' 'You want everything too fast,' and 'You can't expect things to change overnight.' "

After listening to the group's presentation, a woman with many years of experience in the organization reflected on how younger team members had been excluded. "I always assumed that young, single people without kids were privileged. They were available for overtime shift work which meant more money. They were more promotable because they could move to another site quickly. But I changed my mind when I heard their story. Many are ordered to work holidays, even Christmas Day, because they 'don't have a family who needs them home.' That's not true. They have parents, nieces, cousins, and pets ... they have families too!" This group's presentation caused many of the Change Champions to change their assumptions about life as young people in the organization and rethink how to include them and leverage their talents and skills.

Next, the Black Change Champion group shared their stories of the culture and their hopes for the future. Their drawing revealed several images: a ladder with rungs missing and a single figure at the top, a dollar sign, two hats, and a checked box. Here are a few excerpts from their conversation:

As you move up the organizational ladder, you have fewer friends and people who look like you, which is a lonely world. There are twenty perimeter offices on the fifth and sixth floors in headquarters from our count. And just one of them is occupied by an African American.

We must fit the White mold to make Whites more comfortable—keep our hair straight and overdress compared to our peers. It feels like we pay an extra tax to survive in the culture each day.

I wear two hats: one 9-5 and another when I am home.

Blacks must have all the boxes checked to get a promotion. For our White colleagues, if they are liked, leaders will build an organization around them to support their deficiencies. Whites are given the benefit of the doubt for stretch roles. They are told they can grow into it. But when you are Black, you need to check all the boxes, be the whole package.

They described their vision of a more equitable organization where everyone can grow and succeed but said several stereotypes about Black people would need to be overcome for this to happen. Many Change Champions were surprised and disappointed by the emotional and mental toll organizational life takes on their Black colleagues. These storylines starkly contrasted what many Whites experienced in the organization.

The White women's group also had an awakening. The activity allowed them to see themselves as "one-down" as women in the organization but also "up and privileged" as White people. Initially, they asked, "Why are we being divided by race and gender? Shouldn't all the women be in one group if we must divide up?" Their unspoken assumptions included:

- All women face the same challenges.
- Our friendships will be damaged if we recognize and talk about these differences.

Now they said, "We need to think more about our identity as women in the organization and how it plays to our advantage and disadvantage. It's easy to ignore the White part of our identity. After hearing the other groups' presentations, we cannot assume that all women in the organization are experiencing the same things. We must acknowledge how we may have advanced, leaving equally qualified women of color behind. There is much more we need to learn about our White privilege."

The collective story created by each group in the Perception Exchange reveals the similar experiences of individuals and the challenges—often invisible to those outside of the social identity group—that they must navigate to be successful. The activity opens the dialogue about cultural assumptions that limit inclusion, minimize the existence or value of diversity, or view diversity as a disadvantage, and blame the group that has been negatively affected. It surfaces how the isms (e.g., racism, sexism, classism, ageism, heterosexism) manifest inside the organization[3]. It raises the question about the organization's ability to gain a 360-degree vision of issues and see all the perspectives needed to solve an organization problem or imagine future scenarios.

As the Change Champions talk about their social identity group's experience in the organization and listen to the stories of others, the dialogue continues to transform their frames about different groups within the cohort and the rest of the organization. Dialogic change processes assume that language is a primary means of creating, reinforcing, revealing, and modifying mindsets. Disrupting how people talk about things (and each other) can lead to new ways of thinking and behaving, as shown in this example:

> Faced with the opportunity to expand geographically, an organization aggressively recruited new people, including some people of color and White women, to fill service technician roles historically held by older White men. Several Change Champions, concerned that many new team members in their areas were leaving the organization after only a few months, spoke to their managers about how they saw newcomers treated. Typically, new team members were referred to as "trainee," "newbie," or "rookie" rather than by their name. Even if they had significant field knowledge and experience in their previous organizations, new team members were rarely asked about their prior experience or for their opinions. They were "left on the bench" to listen and learn. Some people of color were even referred to as "Affirmative Action hires," which implied that they were recruited only to meet a diversity quota and were less qualified for the job. What may have been paying your dues in years past was experienced as disrespectful and exclusionary.
>
> The Change Champions invited HR into a dialogue about the issue. HR took notice and asked all the area managers to attend a meeting with people with less than two years with the organization. When they heard similar stories from peo-

3 See "Five Ways Isms Manifest" F. A. Miller, 2003, a diagram adapted from the unpublished work of B. Jackson & R. Hardiman.

ple across the organization, including White men, the managers realized they had to think, speak, and act differently if the organization was to retain new talent. Stereotypes and biases created significant barriers to new people joining and, if left unaddressed, would create a lack of interaction safety, low trust, and continued microaggressions. The current storylines that had managers automatically judge new team members as less confident, less able to handle challenging assignments, and less willing to offer innovative ideas and solutions had to shift to a new narrative that included more inclusive ways of talking about and treating newcomers for the organization to meet its goals for growth and to retain talented new people.

A Joining Mindset

The impact of mindsets can be seen in our fundamental orientation toward others. People with a judging mindset will hear others with doubt, engage cautiously, size others up as competitors, and find fault. That places distance between people and limits the person being judged, who often becomes guarded and mistrustful without the interaction safety needed to do their best work and contribute their full range of capabilities and experiences. If people hold a mindset of joining, they will orient themselves toward listening, engaging, and finding ways to partner, collaborate, support, and enhance the contribution of others (Katz & Miller, 2013).

We want Change Champions to learn about and practice a joining mindset that begins with the assumption that the other person has something of value to offer. It is a stance of openness and curiosity toward differences rather than caution and skepticism. It isn't an easy shift for many. Still, when Change Champions experiment with this mindset, they listen more carefully and stay engaged in difficult conversations, which is critical for dialogue and the evolution of the new narrative. That positions the Change Champions to tune into language that minimizes, ignores, or excludes people and their ideas and become more open and curious. They reflect upon and change behaviors that limit how inclusively they interact with others.

Language for More Inclusive Interactions

> Change the language … Change the interaction … Change the result.
>
> —*Fred Miller and Judith Katz,*
> Opening Doors to Teamwork & Collaboration

When people adopt inclusive language, they get different quicker, making it easier to spread new narratives. Using new language is an immediate, palpable way of showing others "I am changing" and can be an invitation for others to get different too. We introduce four Conscious Actions for Inclusion, explicit language which cues more inclusive interactions (Katz & Miller, 2013). Most of this language is familiar to the Change Champions from their cohort ground rules. Now, they shift from using the language as the means to a more productive dialogue in the cohort to a broader, conscious, and deliberate usage to signal to others throughout the organization how they want to be different in their daily interactions. These behaviors are:

- Lean into discomfort.
- Listen as an ally.
- State your intent and intensity.
- Share your street corner.

Lean into Discomfort

Discomfort is a prerequisite to learning, growth, and change. When we *lean into discomfort* in this context, we move toward something new that may be uncomfortable or presents a difficult challenge. This behavior encourages us to challenge ourselves and others to speak up, even if it disrupts the status quo. One of the best ways to model leaning into discomfort is by letting others know when we are doing it. When we use those words, we signal to others, "I am trying something hard for me. I need you to partner with me so I can do this hard thing."

Listen as an Ally

When someone asks you to listen as an ally, the person is asking you to attend as a partner with a joining mindset and give them the benefit of the doubt rather than looking for holes or flaws in their words. When listening as an ally, from the outset of our interaction, we are ready to work a little harder to understand the other person's points of view, support them, and build on their ideas. That opens the door to collaboration and creating a "We." We also want the Change Champions to challenge each other as allies as they work together to construct new narratives and frames.

State Your Intent and Intensity

When we aren't clear about what we mean and how strongly we mean it, we force others to guess our intent, creating the strong possibility that they will guess wrong, which can waste effort, resources, and time. But, when we clearly say what we mean and how committed we are to the idea, others are better able to act quickly, decisively, and correctly. These four metaphors make it easier to clarify the intent and intensity of a message.

- "Here is my *notion*" is an invitation to discuss an initial idea but does not require any action on the listener's part. The listener should only act on a notion if *they,* the listener, think it is helpful.
- "I am putting my *stake* in the ground" communicates a much firmer stance. A stake establishes a starting point for the discussion or idea, but not necessarily where the conversation or action will end. It is grounded in the frame that none of us is as smart as all of us.
- "This is a *boulder* for me" indicates that moving or changing a directive/decision/position will require new, compelling data or a mass of people who push back on the idea or action.
- "This is a *tombstone* for me/us" is a resolute, non-negotiable position. It is a directive or action that is a must-do. Often, these are laws or rules from government agencies or related to individual and organization safety or something that is an organizational imperative from senior leaders.

Share Your Street Corner

Because so many unknowns and unknowables exist in today's organization, getting as many perspectives or street corners as possible to manage challenges and problems is essential. When we ask others to share their street corner, we recognize they have a valuable perspective—that we are standing on one street corner, and we don't have the complete picture of the situation/issue—and accept their viewpoints as valid for them given where they are standing on a different street corner.

Thinking Together with Leaders

> If we can accept that all real change is a shift in narrative—a new story, as opposed to the current lived dominant story—then the function of leadership is to invite a new narrative into existence. Narrative begins with a ride on the wave of conversation. For greatest effect, we need a new conversation with people we are not used to talking to.
>
> *Peter Block,* Community: The Structure of Belonging

Executive Sponsors and senior leaders may want to support greater inclusion, leveraging diversity, equity, and access, but still are figuring out how to live that commitment, show their support to others, and actualize the benefits. Something remarkable happens when Change Champions engage with Executive Sponsors and senior leaders as thinking partners. Their interaction leads to generative questions such as, "What do we want to be different in our new culture?" and "What should we preserve and enhance?" There is the freedom to experiment, express themselves, and embrace ideas that might be "wild" and outside the box of what is.

Creating this dynamic with Change Champions is worth noting since it is rare in most hierarchical organizations for people of different ranks to have a genuine dialogue across their differences. Senge (1990, p. 245) wrote that dialogue could occur "only when a group of people see each other as colleagues in a mutual quest for deeper insight and clarity" and quotes Bohm, who expressed even more strongly that hierarchy is antithetical to dialogue. When Change Champions engage in conversation with senior leaders as partners and colleagues (rather than as their subordinates in a one-down position) and leaders support that approach, the Change Champions don't feel judged, and the dynamic is stimulating and beneficial for both parties. This grows as senior leaders share what they are learning with their peers, the CEO, and the Board.

Many senior leaders say they rediscover their humanness and allow themselves to be vulnerable in the Change Champions' safe container.

Through their interactions with Change Champions, many senior leaders reframe what people can accomplish when unleashed in an organization. Such was the case for two Executive Sponsors who had supported Change Champions for several months.

> High-potential team members were known as "the shiny people" in this organization. Only a select few individuals were considered talented and the most significant contributors. These were the ones who received mentoring, were picked for career-making projects, and put on the fast track for promotion. Several of the Change Champions were not considered shiny people, and there were some concerns when they were selected. But now, the Sponsors and other leaders experienced them as not just workers but as contributors to new ways of thinking and interacting. After a couple of months, they, too, were seen as shiny people.
>
> Change Champions talked and acted differently as they went about their daily work in the organization, modeling some of the inclusive mindsets and behaviors needed in a new culture. When production issues occurred, they asked, "Who else needs to be in the conversation?" which got the right people in the room to explore and solve the problem. When team members from different functions disagreed, they listened as allies and cross-area collaboration increased. They spoke up and encouraged others to speak about hazards, so the organization's safety record improved.
>
> The Sponsors were amazed. They recognized how the Change Champions influenced others and moved the organization toward a new culture. They saw the connection between people interacting differently and better organizational performance. They publicly admitted at a meeting

with Change Champions, "We were wrong. We have a lot of shiny people!" In doing so, they challenged the narrative about talent in the organization. These people had been underestimated. Who else had more to contribute to the organization's success than was assumed? Who else had not even been allowed to contribute? They realized that some current ways of labeling roles, giving feedback, and evaluating performance put people in boxes that limited them and the organization. This made the Executive Sponsors and senior leadership team even more committed to culture change. They already saw the payoff in changing the culture at this initial point in the dialogic process. As one Executive Sponsor said, "Now that I more fully understand the potential impact of Change Champions, I know and welcome how this will change how we operate. It will change the organization as a system."

As the narrative expanded, so did all people's opportunities to contribute more to the organization's success. The Sponsors pledged to take even more decisive action to examine all the organization's formal and informal processes, asking themselves and others, "If every person here—not just a select few—is a valuable talent, a shiny person, what do we need to do differently to be sure everyone feels included and can bring their value?"

Summary

The Change Champions' learning journey requires them to transform their mindsets. Disruptions to personal and organizational narratives lead to experimentation with inclusive language and behaviors, which help new mindsets about inclusion, leveraging diversity, equity, and access emerge and take hold—first within themselves and then throughout the cohort as a group.

Executive Sponsors, Change Champions' managers, and other leaders who join in dialogue also experience disruption as they hear stories of what limits people from doing their best work. Their conversations with Change Champions give them hope for the future and increase their commitment to a Dialogic OD change process. Executive Sponsors are encouraged to notice and share their learnings and experimentation with new mindsets and behaviors with their peers, the CEO, and the

Board. They begin to see a "new normal" in which the process of continually engaging people helps increase the organization's capability to address adaptive challenges and new opportunities.

Checklist for Disrupting and Transforming Mindsets

- ✓ Engage Change Champions in learning activities that help them probe individual and group-level differences and examine personal and organizational mindsets and assumptions.
- ✓ Hold a safe container during difficult conversations so new narratives can emerge.
- ✓ Welcome disruptions as necessary for learning and self-organizing.
- ✓ Introduce a joining mindset and inclusive language.
- ✓ Create opportunities for Change Champions to be thinking partners with Executive Sponsors, senior leaders, and others in the organization.

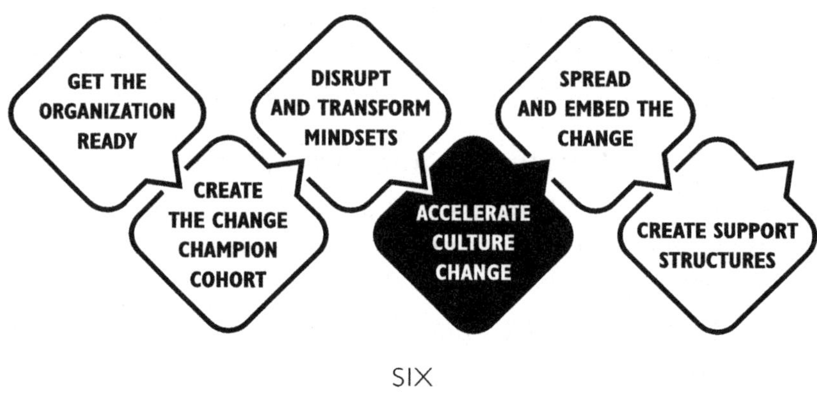

SIX

How Change Champions Accelerate Culture Change

> Nobody can force change on anyone else. It has to be experienced. Unless we invent ways where paradigm shifts can be experienced by large numbers of people, then change will remain a myth
>
> —*Eric Trist, founding member, Tavistock Institute for Social Research*

This chapter focuses on four ways Change Champions accelerate the evolution of a new narrative for the organization by: (a) modeling inclusive mindsets, language, and behaviors in their day-to-day interactions with peers, leaders, and others; (b) leaning into discomfort and taking the risk to intervene in conversations and interactions contrary to the new evolving narratives; (c) sharpening the focus of the culture change into an image of where the organization needs to *evolve from*—mindsets, narratives, language, and cultural artifacts that hold the organization back—and *move to*—what the organization culture aspires to become; and, (d) enrolling groups of allies who partner with Change Champions to spread the new narratives broadly throughout the organization.

Everyday Interactions

When Change Champions intervene in patterns not serving the organization well, even small changes in the conversation can improve information sharing, problem-solving, decision-making, and implementation. We asked Change Champions from several organizations, "How are your everyday interactions impacting team and organization results?" Here are some of their responses which provide examples of what Change Champions do day-to-day:

> Inclusion taught me that if they are okay speaking, the quietest person in the room might be the person to hear from. They often listen and think and have insights that can be valuable to the group. After I shared what inclusion means, team members noticed when others had not spoken and invited quieter people to share their thoughts.
>
> Most of our team are White men who have been in the organization for many years. Our newest three members are women of color. A group norm of saying, "Let me share my street corner" and "I'm leaning into discomfort" has created a sense of safety for our newer members to speak up and offer their ideas and opinions. We're seeing better problem-solving and decision-making as more recent members can contribute sooner.
>
> I am one of four women on my shift. During our shift change, I would hear a few of the other women grumble about an issue, but they wouldn't bring it up to our supervisor, who is a man. I started leaning into my discomfort to speak up, and my issues began to be addressed! This encouraged my women teammates to feel safe talking about problems and opportunities for improvement.
>
> We were approaching an impasse in a supplier meeting when I determined something had to change. I slowed down, stepped back, and asked questions, listening more deeply as an ally. The impasse was resolved, and a great solution was agreed to by both parties, which will provide new SKUs and potentially more than $10 million/year in revenue.
>
> I have been encouraging team members my age to approach managers when they see a problem to get the right people

together and figure out a solution. These team members feel free to use their agency because they are included and feel the agency to move the new narratives forward.

The following three cases show how Change Champions' living the new narrative can positively impact organizational priorities such as quality, safety, and production. Change Champions addressed a class divide in the first case, resulting in more efficient problem-solving. In the second case, safety was enhanced when a Change Champion leaned into discomfort to speak up and move an improvement forward. And in the third case, a Change Champion initiated a dialogue to avoid a lay-off when production demands dropped.

Collaborating Across a "Class" Divide

Like most organizations that experience rapid growth, job roles became differentiated based on perceived knowledge, skills, and experience needed to perform the tasks. While differentiated job roles improved efficiency and coordination of work tasks, some groups were judged as better, not just different, from other groups. The engineers with advanced degrees were the "up" or privileged group. Although most operators had a high-school diploma or a few years of college and many years of experience, whenever there was a production issue on the line, they were told to stop work, immediately call the engineering team, explain the problem, and take a break while the manager and the engineer tried to solve the problem. Time, money, and effort were wasted as the engineers tried to sort out the problem without the operators' insight into the root cause or how to address it.

Among the cohort of Change Champions were several operators and a few engineers. This situation came up in a dialogue about group-level differences and the lack of inclusion of operators in shop floor problem-solving. The engineers were surprised to learn how excluded the operators felt; it was difficult for them to hear how their attitude and language communicated a lack of respect for the operators' knowledge and experience. Although relatively few of the breakdowns were due to human error, the operators felt blamed. The operators strongly believed they had equally valuable perspectives to contribute to problem-solving. They acknowledged the engineers' analytical skills but were critical of what they perceived as their lack of hands-on experience. An intense conversation ended with both groups apologizing for how they had perceived the other group's value. Both said they were ready to work for the common good. Everyone wanted the production line to work smoothly. What emerged from their dialogue was a plan to initiate joint problem-solving with engineers and operators. They piloted it on one shift and line. It was common practice within a few months across several production lines, providing more creative and faster solutions to fixing malfunctions.

Not all the class distinctions that separated these two groups were erased. However, their dialogue generated a new image of problem-solving on the production floor. Operators were not "pairs of hands." They had experience-based insights and information to solve problems expeditiously. And engineers were not just people with degrees without practical experience who looked down on others. The collaboration between engineers and operators opened possibilities for more creative solutions.

Increasing Team Member Safety

Mechanics were experiencing hand injuries while performing maintenance activities in classified Clean Room spaces. Per the organization's standard operating procedures and the procurement process, no gloves had been found that provided the required level of hand protection. Upon raising their concern, the mechanics were told they should be more careful about their work. But George, a lead mechanic and Change Champion, had learned to lean into his discomfort, speak up, and challenge the status quo.

"I took a chance at an industry safety fair, talked to a vendor, and found a protective glove suitable for classified spaces. I almost backed out when I realized I would have to push back on procurement and obtain approval from senior leaders in three different functions to have the glove authorized. But inside, I knew this was exactly what I was supposed to do based on what we were saying in the new narrative. It took some time, and it wasn't easy setting up meetings and talking to top leaders, but eventually, I got approval, and now we are using the gloves throughout the plant."

George's initiative significantly improved a site-wide goal to improve hand safety. By modeling the behaviors of the desired new narrative, such as speaking up and working for the common good and shared success, his actions helped change the storyline that innovative solutions only originated from quality leaders and senior leaders. He demonstrated that innovation could come from anyone in the organization; he showed his peers that the leadership team would listen and support change, even from him.

Avoiding a Lay-off

The production timelines for a Redi-pen injected vaccine were reduced by half, which meant fewer operators were needed on the shop floor in that area. In the past, this situation would trigger a lay-off of operators based on tenure, with the loss of newer team members. Tara, the Integrated Product Team Lead and a Change Champion, got the leadership team's support to develop a solution that would achieve a smooth transition with maximum buy-in from the group.

She invited representatives from the operator group, shift supervisors, and other staff to a dialogue session to solve the problem. The dialogue was messy, and feelings ran high, but people leaned into discomfort and listened as allies to focus on meeting the organization's needs while retaining operators. The group developed a synchronized shift configuration that would meet the production goal and included cross-skills training to build flexibility to meet future demands. Opportunities to transfer four team members with the requisite skills and experience to other production areas were also identified. Joined by the leadership team, the Redi-pen team's experiment with a new narrative, "Together we can adapt to changing conditions and solve workforce issues," successfully resolved a complex problem with buy-in from the affected people.

Joining "Resisters"

Engaging peers (and sometimes leaders) using new mindsets, language, and ways of interacting can be met with skepticism, criticism, or ridicule. When this happens, Change Champions often need to be coached not to ignore, fight, or discount resistance but to reframe it as data and information to be curious about and recognize that people manifest different energies throughout the change process. If they avoid labeling and judging people, Change Champions can hear those who have skepticism or criticism or ridicule for the effort more clearly and find ways for new narratives to include the self-interest of even the most resistant team members.

Semi, a plant manager and Change Champion Executive Sponsor, faced significant resistance in a collective bargaining session with union representatives. The following describes his experimentation with inclusive behaviors that supported the new narrative about unions and management working for the common good.

> Historically, bargaining sessions were tense conversations. Any concession by the union generated feelings of resentment and reinforced an "us versus them" attitude. Union reps and management lined up on opposite sides of the table, not showing any emotion and not extending any welcome—just looking across the table at each other, preparing to have their "buttons pushed" by the other side. Despite a new, evolving narrative that union and management would work for the common good—and, admittedly, both sides wanted the plant, a prominent local employer, to prosper—the long-held narrative that union and management were adversaries prevailed at the start of the bargaining session.
>
> But on this day, Semi was ready to be different. Talking with the Change Champions in their sessions opened his eyes as an Executive Sponsor. He learned how people could change and how the plant needed to listen to and support different views to achieve higher plant results. "Instead of taking my designated place at the table, I entered the room, walked around, and said hello to each person authentically and warmly. I then sat on the union 'side' of the table. It shocked them. When asked what I was doing by sitting on their 'side,' I responded, 'Don't we all want the same thing

here? I think we both want what is best for the plant and the people who work here. And, in that sense, we are both on the same side.' Still in shock, but getting my point, the negotiations started."

Semi continued disrupting expectations and challenging assumptions about collective bargaining throughout the session. He enacted the new narrative, "We all want the same thing here: what is best for the plant and our people," using an inclusive mindset and language developed through the Change Champion process. Acknowledging the tendency in collective bargaining sessions to polarize issues, he asked, "Let's keep the focus on the mission and values of our organization and make the culture changes that are best for the organization's success and for creating team higher performance." He then listened as an ally rather than an adversary and asked questions to better understand the union's position. He said, "I'm leaning into discomfort" when the conversation became tense; he explained management's stakes and boulders. He stayed open to the union representatives' stakes and boulders and sought places for compromise and agreement. Overall, the environment became much less confrontational. Union representatives and management had an honest and straightforward dialogue that day and the days following. They eventually agreed to a contract that both sides described as "the best we have ever had."

Generating an Image of the Future

> As I think about moving the culture to adapt to massive changes in our industry, we need a community of effort.
>
> —*CEO, major international airline*

For this leader, a *community of effort* was a generative image of a high-performing organization, i.e., a group of people working together across their differences, including roles and levels, to meet adaptive challenges and accomplish the organization's mission and strategic initiatives. We find it a generative image as well. When the whole organization is engaged as a community of effort, people become more willing to experiment with new mindsets and behaviors and "multiple strands of shared meaning begin to bind the organization together" (Senge et al., 1994, p. 300). This creates what Block (2018) calls a structure of belonging, which is more critical for generative change than a formal vision or plan.

In the generative change model, Bushe (2020) describes purpose as "what we are trying to do every day" and distinguishes that from a vision, which is one way to accomplish a purpose. An inspiring purpose is necessary for more emergent approaches to transformational change. Bushe promotes the use of "generative images" (Bushe, 2020; Bushe & Storch, 2015), which are unusual combinations of words that produce an appealing, ambiguous image that helps people think and act differently than they could have imagined before.

We use a structure we call FROM→TOs. The FROM→TOs sharpen the picture of the desired future based on what people have said they need and want in daily interactions and what the organization needs to transform and thrive. We have found that identifying and stating where the organization needs to evolve *from*—mindsets, storylines, language, and cultural artifacts that hold it back—and what it aspires to move *to* can be a powerful and clear statement of the needed change and the new narratives that everyone is expected to live. The new narrative includes those aspects of the current culture that need to be kept, sustained and strengthened (Schein & Schein, 2019).

Creating FROM→TOs

During their education sessions, Change Champions propose initial FROM→TOs to frame the new narratives. Their thinking is grounded in what was heard in the Giving Voice dialogues at the start of the culture change process, in their own experiences in the organization, and what they have learned by listening and interacting with peers and others in the organization. The Change Champions share the draft FROM→TOs with Executive Sponsors, other leaders, thinking partners, and allies. Together, they talk about how the FROM→TOs align with the new narratives to support the accomplishment of the organization's mission, vision, values, and goals. Changes are made throughout the process as needed.

In partnership with leaders and other allies, the Change Champions share the next draft of the FROM→TOs throughout the organization in dialogue sessions and informal conversations with large and small groups. They collect feedback from these sessions about how well the FROM→TOs capture the core cultural issues limiting inclusion, leveraging diversity, equity, and access, and they modify the drafts accordingly. Through this iterative process, the FROM→TOs become a mechanism for developing shared meaning about the organization's future vision and help more people commit to living the new narratives. Here's an example from one company.

Vulcan-ized

Vulcan was a successful materials distributor that prided itself on its strong service culture fostered by people who closely guarded organizational know-how and cultural traditions. Team members with different experiences, skills, styles, and backgrounds eagerly suggested different ways of working but were typically told, "Slow down! That's not how we do things here. You and your ideas need to be Vulcan-ized first." However, the complexity of global supply chains and unexpected breakdowns in distribution channels created a level of risk never faced by the organization in its century of operation. If Vulcan was going to maintain its market position, everyone needed to be problem solvers and workflow improvers, experimenting with and collaborating on new, quicker ways to meet customer needs.

The Change Champions who carried a new narrative were initially met with protests: "Not everything about being Vulcan-ized is bad!" But, while the prevailing assumptions about "Vulcan-izing" provided a sense of communal identity and stability, bonding people to the organization's mission, and helping coordinate its activities, they also stymied an organization that needed to adapt and innovate to thrive in a changing world. The FROM→TOs (Table 6-1) offered a new image of "Vulcan-izing" as engaging everyone's full capabilities to anticipate problems and experiment with bolder solutions to meet customer needs. The new image of "Vulcan-izing" also included what people said already existed in the current culture and needed to be reinforced and supported as the new narrative takes hold.

Table 6-1: Proposed FROM→TOs (New Narratives) for Vulcan

From	To
Traditional ways of working are to be preserved. Different ideas and ways of working threaten our organizational identity.	Experimentation with new ways of working is essential to our success. Differences enhance and strengthen our organizational identity.
Team members' differences are a problem to be overcome or managed.	Team members' unique ideas, skills, and talents are valued and encouraged.
Trust is earned over time.	Trust is automatically and rapidly extended.
Keep	
We deliver on our commitments.	
Problems are made visible and solved at the root cause.	

Ping Surveys

With many clients we use ping surveys to measure the organization's progress toward actualizing the new narrative, including how it shows up in people's actions. A ping is a short, scaled survey (sometimes including open-ended questions) that provides data about where the organization is on the path to gaining critical mass[4] for the new narrative. The TOs are helpful for constructing these.

One-third of the organization is surveyed every other month, with individuals participating in two pings per year. The saying, "What gets

4 Critical mass or the tipping point is the critical point in an organization change effort beyond which a significant and often unstoppable effect or change takes place. In the context of organizational culture change, it is the point at which the new narratives are prevalent enough to sustain the culture. At critical mass, many of the organization's systems, structures, and processes are aligned with the new narratives, and higher performance and other expected benefits are beginning to be realized.

measured, gets done," holds true in most organizations, so the pings can be powerful influences on the change process. A ping sets expectations for action, so positioning and organizational communication are essential before and after the ping is deployed. HR and/or the Executive Sponsors announce and administer the ping and share the results with the organization. It is important to prepare leaders to expect ratings to dip (as shown in Table 6-2 ping 2) as people become clearer about the new narratives, and their expectations for change rise, and before change happens. The most important thing about ping results is they provide an opportunity to regularly dialogue about the change. As people know, data doesn't speak for itself, it is interpreted, and it is the process of sharing interpretations that deserves most attention. Bratt (2020) offers a dialogic approach to discuss survey data results.

Tables 6-2 and 6-3 show a sample of ping survey results for two organizations. In Table 6-2, for the change in scores from Baseline to Ping 3 to be statistically significant with 80% confidence, the change interval needs to be 6 or greater. We have seen organizations move to high 90s on all or most dimensions.

Table 6-2: Sample Ping Mean Scores for Organization 1[5]

Question	Baseline Survey	Ping 1	Ping 2	Ping 3	Change between Baseline & Ping 3
I am seeing people use inclusion to improve interactions and performance.	51	64	63	74	+23

5 In Organization 1, an organization-wide survey was administered at the start of the culture change process. These results provided a baseline against which to measure progress in subsequent pings.

We operate under the assumption that everyone here is working toward the best interest of the organization.	64	71	69	77	+13
People have access to the information they need to do their best work.	58	63	64	70	+12
When we challenge ideas in my work group/ team, we do it respectfully.	77	79	77	85	+8
My coworkers actively seek out different perspectives when solving problems.	68	72	67	74	+6
I feel comfortable sharing my ideas with others.	72	77	72	78	+6

Table 6-3: Sample Ping Mean Scores for Organization 2

Question	Ping 1	Ping 2	Ping 3	Change between Pings 1 & 3
People in my work group try to apply inclusive mindsets, language, and behaviors in their interactions.	38	69	69	+31
I have started to see examples of linkages between inclusion and better teamwork, collaboration, and problem solving.	62	70	75	+13
We lean into discomfort, challenging ourselves and others.	61	68	70	+9
We ask who else needs to be included to understand the whole situation to ensure right people, right work, right time.	64	70	72	+8
People put problems on the table, making them visible.	64	59	71	+7

Accelerating Change with Pods

The organization takes a big step toward adopting the new narratives when the Change Champions invite a group of six to eight allies to form a Pod. This happens midway through the Change Champion's education series. By then, the Change Champions have started to intervene in day-to-day interactions and need allies to support them to continue expanding the adoption of the new narratives. Pod members serve two primary purposes. One is to accelerate the adoption of the new narratives throughout the organization by changing conversations, one after another, creating a ripple effect. The other is to act as a support system for the Change Champions on the front line of the culture change effort by "having their back" and advocating for and experimenting with the new narratives.

In partnership with the Change Champions, Pod members learn how to bring the behaviors and language of the new narratives into their work interactions. They agree to support Change Champion's efforts to practice and live the new narratives, i.e., "have their back." They act as early adopters of and advocates for the new narratives and help enroll their peers to adopt the new narratives.

This peer-to-peer partnership, collaboration, and leadership model accelerates change in several ways. First, it creates an *ad hoc network* where spontaneous connection and communication promote the distribution and uptake of the new narratives (Miller & Davis-Howard, 2022). Second, although sanctioned by leaders as part of the change process, this network operates outside the formal organizational structure, encouraging the Change Champions and Pod members to self-organize and reap the benefits of emergence. Using a generative, "learning as you go" approach by staying in contact and dialogue, and encouraging numerous, simultaneous experimental initiatives with their peers results in far more rapid change (Bushe, 2020). Lastly, a "pull" effect is created by the many simultaneous interactions of Change Champions and Pod members with their peers and others versus the traditional "push" from the organization's top. Others sign up because they are attracted to what they hear and see. If their message and behavior resonate, a critical mass of people experimenting with components of the new narratives will emerge and transform the culture.

We give the following guidance to Change Champions as they form their Pod:

- Choose Pod members who are willing to influence their peers to experiment with the new narratives; are eager to learn, grow, and change; and represent a mix of demographic and social identity groups, such as tenure, age, organizational levels, race/ethnicity, gender identities, and life experiences/backgrounds.
- Meet with your Pod every two weeks. Plan on two-hour meetings at the beginning, during Phases 1 and 2 (Figure 6-1). As the Pod

evolves, move to sixty- to ninety-minute meetings. Pods typically continue meeting for nine to twelve months, depending on how soon the adoption of new mindsets and narratives reaches critical mass.

- Institute norms such as "hellos," check-ins, ground rules, and honoring confidentiality to create interaction safety in Pod meetings.
- Use Pod meetings to:
    - o Transfer knowledge to members about inclusion and the new narratives.
    - o Experiment with inclusive mindsets, language, and behaviors.
    - o Support and offer advice to each other.
    - o Share signs of the new narratives adding value to interactions and results.
- Have Pod members convey messages about the culture change effort to Executive Sponsors and other senior leaders.
- Invite managers and others to meetings to learn and dialogue with your Pod.

Evolution of Peer-to-Peer Partnership

A Pod typically moves through four phases, although the process is not as linear as Figure 6-1 depicts. Most of the phases overlap.

Figure 6-1: Evolution of a Pod

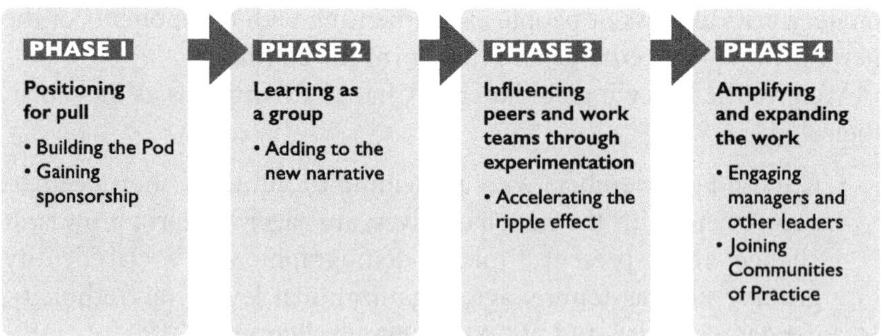

Phase 1: Positioning for Pull

Positioning the Pods to create "pull" and attract people to join the effort begins with Executive Sponsors letting the organization know that Change Champions will be forming Pods. We suggest Pod members come from their organizational unit and represent a range of levels and functions. The Change Champion (and/or their manager) will have to meet with the potential Pod members' manager(s) to gain the manager's support for the expected time commitment, and request the employee have a say in the decision to join the Pod while answering the manager's questions and concerns. It may be necessary to offer the managers some education on the Change Champion goals and process and their role in supporting Pod members.

Supporting the Pod Member

Managers can support and be an ally to the Pod members from their area/department in several ways. They can ask Pod members what they are learning and encourage them to experiment with new language and behaviors in their team and in other places where they have influence. We want managers to be open to new ways of thinking and doing that may enhance individual and team performance; support inclusion and leverage diversity, and directly address issues and conflicts that emerge; and be willing to join some Pod meetings and show appreciation for the learning and experimentation that the Pod member is doing. They can also communicate to peers how vital the Change Champion and Pod members' roles are in creating a new narrative and ask everyone to support them.

The First Pod Meeting

In the first meeting, we ask Change Champions to talk about their role as a change agent and ask Pod members to give them feedback if they are not speaking up with courage and candor to leaders, peers, and others in the organization. In turn, we encourage the Change Champion to be explicit about what they need from Pod members. We call this a "cover my back agreement" that could include things like speaking up for me when others are talking me down, joining me in feedback discussions with leaders, and learning enough that you can explain why the organization is investing in the creation of a new narrative that will lead to a new culture that's more inclusive.

Phase 2: Learning as a Group

If it progresses, the Pod becomes a learning community with guidance from the Change Champion. The Change Champion teaches Pod members inclusive mindsets, language, behaviors, and the FROM→TOs that frame the new narratives. They dialogue about what they see in the organization that needs to change and how the new narratives can address those challenges and opportunities. The Change Champion shares their experience intervening in day-to-day interactions. The Pod discusses how to manage the risk of speaking up to leaders, peers, and others in the organization as the new narratives and frames are spread. This phase typically lasts for four to six months.

Phase 3: Influencing Peers and Work Teams

If the Pod members are vigorously using inclusive mindsets, language, and behaviors that support the new narratives, responsibility for the Pod becomes shared. They discuss what they are seeing and experiencing and how they and others can apply the emerging narratives to more situations, challenges, and opportunities. The Change Champion still convenes the meetings, but Pod members co-create the agenda and share the facilitation.

Phase 4: Amplifying and Expanding the Work

Finding ways to bring all the Pods together from time to time helps expand and amplify their collective efforts. These can be designed in different ways to learn from each other, tackle system-wide issues, celebrate successes and reaffirm commitments. Table 6-4 shows a typical agenda from one of our "Pod Days."

Table 6-4: Example of a Pod Day Design

- Welcome from CEO and Executive Sponsors
- Purpose and flow of the day
- Ground rules for the day
- Hellos

Table 6-4 continued

• Connecting Activity: People share their responses question by question, beginning in pairs and combining group to group until they are in large groups of sixteen. For example: o Round 1 (in pairs): What is one thing that excites you these days? What are two "gifts"/attributes/qualities that you bring to interactions with others? o Round 2 (pairs join to form groups of four): What are two things you have gained from practicing the mindsets, language, and behaviors of the new narratives and/or being on this learning journey o Round 3 (groups of four join to form groups of eight): As the organization moves forward with living the new narrative, what will be the most challenging part about continuing, accelerating, and enhancing how people interact or work together? What will be the easiest part o Round 4 (groups of eight join to form groups of sixteen): What are two actions or behaviors you have done to live the new narrative o Round 5 (the entire group): What will the organization gain by living the new narrative? • Group dialogue to share highlights and reactions from the conversations and take the collective pulse of the entire group.
• Review the results of the latest ping tracking adoption of the new narratives and the FROM→TOs. • Form small groups (each a mix of supervisors/managers, Change Champions, and Pod members). Each group focuses on one of the following topics: 1. Supervisor/Managers: What four to five actions would accelerate supervisors' and managers' ability to experiment with the new narratives? Are there parts of the new narrative that you would suggest supervisors and managers experiment with more?

Table 6-4 continued

Review Small Groups (cont) 8. Change Champions/Pod Members: What four to five actions would increase the influence and effectiveness of Change Champions and Pod members? What parts of the new narrative need to be adopted more fully? In what areas/groups in the organization? 9. Our Performance: What two to three actions could the CEO and senior leaders experiment with to enhance the application of the new narratives to meet the organization's key metrics? • Presentations and open dialogue with the whole group to synthesize and commit to next steps and add any thoughts and/or images to the new narrative.
• Announce when Pods will come together next.
• Closing comments with final words from the most senior leader.

Communities of Practice

Pods evolve into Communities of Practice when organizational benefits from living the new narratives begin to be realized, as measured by ping surveys and critical performance metrics such as quality, turnover, customer satisfaction, revenue, cost reductions, and delivery time (Wenger, 1998). Chapter Seven describes the indicators we use to help the organization determine its tipping point for change.

Organizations may establish site-wide, functional, organization-wide, and global Communities of Practice that convene virtually and in person. A Community of Practice may meet quarterly or more frequently for members to share examples of how the new narratives support higher performance and engage in dialogue to continually challenge the status quo to adapt to ever-changing conditions.

Summary

Change Champions intervene daily in patterns of interaction that do not serve the organization well. We offered several examples of how even small changes in the conversation can support greater inclusion and leveraging of differences that improve information sharing, problem-solving, decision-making, and higher performance at all levels.

Clear images of the desired future based on what people have said they need and want, and what the organization needs to transform and thrive are required. We described the FROM→TOs method we use to accomplish that. An advantage of FROM→TOs is they are a good source of items for ping surveys to track progress and catalyze ongoing dialogues.

Change Champions form networks of allies called Pods to accelerate the adoption of the new narratives through their willingness to experiment with and model new mindsets, language, and behaviors and encourage others to adopt them. Pod members join others to form Communities of Practice to sustain the momentum for change and continuously challenge the status quo.

Checklist for Change Champions to Accelerate Culture Change

- ✓ With the Change Champions, create clear statements of the desired future to sharpen the focus of the new narratives and accompanying behaviors.
- ✓ Use these as the basis for dialogue sessions with sponsors, managers, thinking partners, and later Pods.
- ✓ Collect feedback from these sessions about how well the desired futures capture the core cultural issues limiting inclusion, leveraging diversity, equity, and access, and modify the drafts accordingly.
- ✓ Use ping surveys to measure the organization's progress toward actualizing new narratives, including changes in how people interact.
- ✓ Give Change Champions a process for enrolling Pod members who will accelerate the embedding of new narratives.
- ✓ Get Sponsor agreement on how Change Champions (or their managers) can contract with Pod members' supervisors and managers so they can fully participate.
- ✓ Utilize the Pods to cover the backs of the Change Partners, to be a learning community, and accelerate the change process.
- ✓ Transition Pods into Communities of Practice to sustain the momentum.

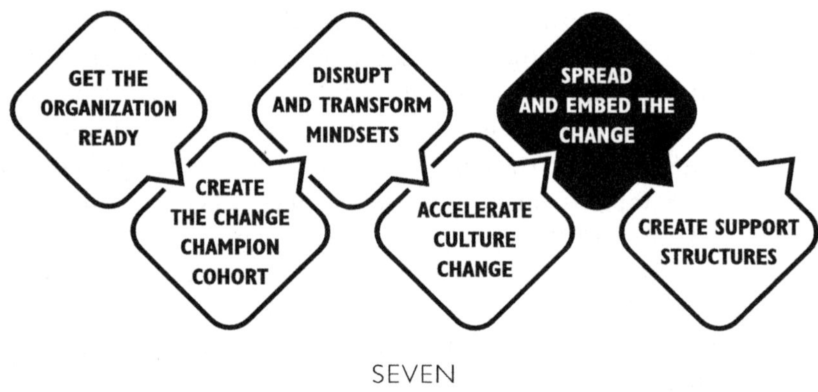

SEVEN

Spreading and Embedding the Change

> The tipping point is that magic moment when an idea, trend, or social behavior crosses a threshold, tips, and spreads like wildfire.
>
> —*Malcolm Gladwell,* The Tipping Point: How Little Things Can Make a Big Difference

Organizations reach critical mass, or the tipping point for change, when the new narrative is embedded in policies and operational procedures and the benefits of the culture change are realized in organizational performance. This chapter describes elements for spreading and embedding the change, including sharing success stories and preparing Human Resources to align people and management systems with the mindsets, language, behaviors, and accountabilities needed in the new narrative. We briefly discuss various ways to help an organization assess when the new narrative is sufficiently institutionalized and likely to sustain.

Stories of Successful Experiments with the New Narrative

When people hear stories of how the organization is changing for the better, it gives them hope. It inspires them to adopt the new narratives, especially when the initial view of the journey and the changes needed seem long and complicated. The practice of sharing success stories does more than "report on or reflect information; it is constructive and establishes, reinforces, and challenges how organizational actors interpret their organizational experiences" (Marshak et al., 2015, pp. 83–84). For example, you can ask a small group of Change Champion volunteers to design and manage a process to capture, compile, and communicate success stories shared and collected from others. They can write articles for internal newsletters and blogs, make short videos using their phones, post on social media, and influence leaders to incorporate success stories into their meetings and day-to-day conversations.

Success stories reflect the new narrative of how the organization is changing. They help track progress toward critical mass for change and boost momentum for continuing the effort. One client, a chemical manufacturer, leveraged the power of sharing success stories at a global summit of 400 leaders:

> The senior leadership team of Chemical Products Inc. believed that greater inclusion and engagement were market differentiators that could drive higher profitability, productivity, and customer satisfaction in an increasingly uncertain global environment. Now, two years into a Dialogic OD cultural transformation, 400 leaders convened a global summit to build additional momentum for their journey to be a more "Inclusive and Engaged Organization." At various points in the summit, leaders shared stories of how the new narratives were taking hold, with examples of how people using inclusive mindsets, language, and behaviors could reduce waste, collaborate on problem-solving, and meet revenue and customer satisfaction goals. Whereas in the past, leaders shared stories of what business results were achieved, now, they discussed HOW those results were achieved through greater inclusion of the right people, listening to different voices, and increased collaboration. Success stories were signs that the new narratives were moving the organizational culture *from* one that treated its people as costs and disposable *to* a culture that treated its people as valuable assets to be nurtured and retained.
>
> Leaders left the summit highly energized to continue to live the new narratives. They formed Engagement Groups as

a monthly forum for learning and sharing successes. A small group of leaders agreed to develop a process for measuring the impact of the "Inclusive and Engaged Organization" effort alongside bottom-line productivity and profitability. This tool, in addition to collecting and disseminating success stories, helped maintain and cement the connection between the enactment of the organization's new narrative and business results.

Embedding Change with Human Resources

In most organizations, Human Resources (HR) "owns" the people and management systems[6] in core areas such as recruitment and hiring, talent management, training and development, performance management, compensation and benefits, and safety and compliance. These systems reflect the culture and shape how people conduct themselves and how work gets done.

Peter Drucker famously said "the greatest danger in times of turbulence is not the turbulence itself, but to act with yesterday's logic," such as twentieth-century mindsets and narratives about people. Many traditional HR policies and practices are based on outmoded attitudes, at odds with developing highly inclusive organizations able to leverage diversity. Here are a few examples:

- People are human resources to be used and replaced as needed.
- Career success looks like a bus route with many required stops. If you sit in the right seat for the proper time, you might reach your destination.
- People who are a "good fit" are the best hires. The new hire's job is to mold themselves to fit with the rest of us.
- New people should be quiet and listen and just do their jobs until they have been with the organization for a couple of years.
- Most people only care about how much they are paid; they will live with other less desirable factors if the pay is right for them.

---

6 People and management systems include organizational structures and processes. Structures define how work is divided and coordinated, including how roles are designed, authority is allocated, and how people are expected to interact. Processes are formal and informal aspects of the organization that guide behavior, including procedures, rules, norms, and cultural values and beliefs.

- Following the chain of command is the most effective way to accomplish things, so communication should not skip levels.
- The fairest approach to HR policies and practices is one-size-fits-all.
- Addressing cultural bias and dehumanizing behaviors is the job of the HR and Legal departments.

A Parallel Learning Journey

HR needs to understand not just the mindsets, language, and behaviors that drive inclusion and support diversity, equity, and access in the new narrative but also how people and management systems unintentionally formalize and institutionalize bias and other barriers that impact how people interact and are treated by the organization. To prepare for their work to review, revise, and align people and management systems, the Human Resources team will need to engage in a learning process like the Change Champions, although less time intensive. We use a dialogic approach to engage HR leaders and HR Subject Matter Experts (SMEs) in a four-session education and application series (Table 7-1) in which they:

- Explore mindsets underlying current systems which may be outmoded, such as those listed earlier.
- Learn how the Change Champions and other allies are changing interactions within the organization and how leadership needs to be different to support the new narrative.
- Learn from Change Champions what systems are barriers to a more inclusive, diverse, equitable organization.
- Decide what and how to change or enhance in current systems to align with the emerging narrative and frame for the organization.
- Apply mindsets, language, and behaviors needed in the emerging new reality to their area of HR specialty and interactions with each other and the organization.

Table 7-1: Positioning Human Resources to Co-create and Support a New Narrative

Objectives	• Develop further understanding and skills to enable HR to create and change systems, processes, and competencies to support inclusion, leverage diversity, and increase equity and access. • Gain knowledge and expand capability so the HR function can embed the mindsets and behaviors of the new narrative into their areas of responsibility (e.g., HR strategy planning, compensation and benefits, performance management systems, community outreach, talent recruitment, etc.).
Process	• Four two-day sessions held over three months.

Examples of questions that can frame the dialogue include:

- Which of our existing HR and management policies, processes, structures, and programs enable people to do their best work and the organization to be higher and higher performing? Why?
- What new or changed HR and management policies, processes, structures, and programs, if adopted, would assist us in living the new narrative—a new way of interacting so that everyone can do their best work?
- What else do we need to consider regarding HR and management policies, processes, structures, and programs to position, support, and sustain the new narrative?

Examples of the actions that HR groups can take to align with and support the new narratives include:

- Ensure that recruitment, interviewing, and hiring processes are inclusive. Check that algorithms used to find candidates are bias-free, gender decode job descriptions, and hold hiring managers accountable for unbiased evaluation of job candidates.

- Share the FROM→TOs with recruiters so they understand the evolving culture to attract a broader group of candidates.
- Analyze individual and group-level compensation and create strategies for adjusting to ensure equitable pay and promotion rates.
- Review reward and recognition practices to support and encourage behaviors related to the new narratives.
- Train leaders to use nonbiased strategies to identify team members with a high potential for organizational promotion and leadership.
- Formalize accountability for living the new narratives with a scorecard.

Roadblocks

Typically, Human Resources leaders want to support the Dialogic OD process and the Change Champion intervention. When we experience roadblocks to forming a partnership with HR, it's usually one of four issues. 1) HR is not positioned to effect system change. The organization may see HR team members as order-takers, performing transactional tasks on behalf of managers, e.g., screening candidates but having little or no voice in the hiring decision. 2) HR sees its role as preservers and protectors of the status quo, *not* agents of change, and is unwilling to support the development of internal change agents such as Change Champions. 3) HR sees the Change Champions as competition for resources, projects, or initiatives. 4)The HR function is siloed, with little sense of the whole; each area in HR may have competing goals. If you experience a reluctance to engage with the Dialogic OD change process, meet with the HR senior leadership team to figure out what is causing their unwillingness. Work with them to develop strategies to mitigate or remove roadblocks. Here's an example.

> In a large municipal government client, the HR leadership team was sitting on the sidelines, waiting for the culture change effort to encounter setbacks that would lead to its cancellation. After several conversations, we learned that they had been "beaten down" repeatedly when they tried to lead culture change in the past. No one in city leadership would support them. Pessimistic that any change effort

would succeed, they resorted to putting down change efforts so as not to waste their or the organization's time.

We facilitated a meeting with HR leaders, the City Manager, and City Council members to hear and understand the reason for HR's skepticism and reluctance to support the change process. After listening and reflecting on what he heard, the City Manager apologized for past failures to support HR and then offered his perspective about why this cultural transformation, at this time, was needed to serve city residents more effectively: "I believe our culture impacts every action citizens have with city government. It's how you're taxed, how your kids get schooled, whether potholes get filled, what it's like to report a crime, and how your neighborhood gets zoned. Our culture is at the root of all these experiences. Culture change is critical to getting the type of municipal government our residents expect and deserve."

He and the council members pledged their active sponsorship of the Dialogic OD process and directly asked for HR's support. After one more meeting in which components of the Dialogic OD process were outlined and the role of HR in the process was discussed, negotiated, and agreed upon, the HR leaders fully joined the change effort and became vital partners in its success.

Critical Mass or the Tipping Point

Also known as the tipping point, critical mass in organizational culture change is the point at which the new narratives have sufficient momentum to continue to be practiced, spread, and sustained in the culture. At critical mass, many of the organization's systems, structures, and processes are aligned, or in the process of being aligned, with the new narratives, and higher performance, and other expected benefits are beginning to be realized. To sustain momentum for the change, it is useful for organizations to measure their progress toward critical mass. Some ways we have done this include periodic ping surveys tracking groups' progress toward adopting the new narratives and the FROM→TOs. Success stories provide examples of how more inclusive interactions result in different, better results. We develop metrics for behaviors and skills needed in the new culture in performance management and reward systems and we track improvements in organizational metrics such as customer satisfaction, on-time delivery of services and products, cost reduction, etc.

Summary

There are several elements for spreading and embedding the change. Success stories build momentum to sustain the change effort. Change Champions develop mechanisms for collecting and disseminating success stories, increasing momentum for change. Engaging Human Resource leaders to identify and implement strategies to reframe, refine, and realign HR and management systems with the new narratives is essential to embed the new culture fully. Finally, these elements, combined with periodic ping surveys and other metrics important to the organization, can help indicate when the tipping point has been achieved and change is likely to be irreversible.

Checklist for Spreading and Embedding the Change

- ✓ Develop a process for Change Champions to collect and communicate success stories of how the new narratives are moving the organization toward achieving its mission, vision, and goals.
- ✓ Partner with HR to upskill leaders and Subject Matter Experts in mindsets, language, and behaviors needed in the new narrative.
- ✓ Support efforts to align HR and management systems with the new narrative.
- ✓ Use ping survey results, success stories, and organizational performance metrics to indicate that the tipping point has been achieved and that change is likely to be sustainable.

EIGHT

Supporting Change Champions During the Change Process

> In easy times and in tough times, what seems to matter most is the way we show those nearest us that we've been listening to their needs, their joys, and their challenges.
>
> —*Fred Rogers, television host and author*

Their education helps Change Champions build skills, resources, and partnerships with people throughout the organization. Still, they confront dilemmas in their change agent role and need support systems to "stay alive." We are reminded that organizations change emergently through what Ralph Stacey calls the "many, many local interactions of all involved, in the many interplays of intention" and that "just what will emerge is uncertain and will continue to produce surprises, some of which will not be wanted by anyone" (2015, p. 157). This chapter focuses on the support structures that can assist Change Champions to "stay alive" and keep learning during and after their "formal" education sessions. We examine how they use their support systems to manage challenges and dilemmas.

Staying Alive

We encourage you to set aside time in every education session for Change Champions to talk about their experiences. Everyone benefits from the wisdom of the cohort as they figure out how to manage change and challenge what is. Their opening comments often sound like this:

> When I told my team I was a Change Champion, some laughed and said, "Sorry about that." On a positive note, in the dialogue sessions, I have seen more people slow down to listen to each other.

> Some of my team members want to know how I will account for my time here. I think a few of them believe this is just me doing some non-value-added activity. That's frustrating.

> My manager wanted to know what I was doing in a meeting with Joe, our Executive Sponsor. I think she is nervous that I might be "telling on her" since Joe is also the vice president of our function. I could use some advice about what to say when I meet with her. I am worried about how my participation as a Change Champion will affect my relationship with her.

> The good news is that I am getting great people to join my Pod. I am hoping to invite the quality manager in my area, too. He talks positively about our change effort and seems ready to influence others to change. Do you think that's a good idea?

Change Champions can get confused, impatient, excited, discouraged, and overwhelmed at many junctures in the change effort. As Herb Shepard (1975) advised, change agents must first stay alive. Staying alive means taking care of yourself—physically and mentally—and staying in touch with your personal and work purposes. One of the ways Change Champions stay alive is to build and rely upon a social support system.

Support structures should provide ways for Change Champions to surface problems and challenges quickly and receive the type of support that serves them and the situation best. You can use several structures to support Change Champions during and after their formal education. The kind of support structures we like to use include:

Lifelines. We ask each Change Champion to identify a partner in the cohort who will be their lifeline and can be contacted 24/7 to help with a problem or listen supportively.

Support Groups. The Change Champions create small groups in the cohort who will provide a willing ear, give advice and feedback at designated times, and share success stories at each education session.

Pods. The Change Champion's Pod members provide ongoing support and feedback. By transferring knowledge and skills, the Change Champion continues to develop the Pod members' capacity to support them in interactions in meetings and with the Pod members' peers and leaders.

Monthly Working Sessions. After the formal education series concludes, we provide Change Champions with monthly working sessions to share their Pod's progress, enhance their inclusive interaction skills, continue to share success stories, coach each other, and dialogue with their managers and senior leaders about what still needs to change in the system.

Communities of Practice. As we described earlier, once the culture change reaches critical mass you can shift from Pods to Communities of Practice located by site, function, organization, or globally, where they find opportunities to continue their learning, connect with cohort members, engage in dialogue with allies, and receive ongoing support and encouragement to live the new narratives.

Managing Dilemmas

By leveraging their support systems, Change Champions can decide how and when to take action to manage dilemmas. Some dilemmas are best handled by recontracting and others by reframing (i.e., how we can look at this situation differently). Here are a few of the common ones we've run into.

Recontracting with Managers

Team workloads change. A Change Champion may face pushback after a few months from their manager about their time commitment. Change Champions often discover that some managers haven't considered how long the change process will take. Usually, things get back on track after talking openly about the expected time commitment in the future and how to manage the Change Champion's workload. If an agreement is not reached, the Change Champion may enlist the support of the Executive Sponsor to re-emphasize the importance of the Change Champion's involvement in the change effort and seek a solution.

It can also be beneficial for the Executive Sponsor to talk to the manager about how being more involved in the change process will benefit them as a leader in the organization. If they are open to it, managers should be welcome to join strategy and working sessions with the Change Champions.

Confronting Negative Appropriations

In one organization, several Change Champions were dismayed to realize that some managers were co-opting the language "I am going to lean into discomfort" as a cover for disrespectful or unproductive interactions—shifting its meaning to "What I am going to say will create discomfort for you." After consulting with their Pod members, the Change Champions met one-on-one with a few managers to discuss the negative consequence of using the language this way. They offered examples of how inclusive language improved team interactions: as people stated that they were leaning into discomfort, problems were made visible quicker, and collaborative problem-solving increased. They asked the managers to reframe how they used the language and share their experiences with their peers. It's a "We" effort.

Overreliance

Change Champions can get burned out if the organization over relies on their efforts. Emphasize that Executive Sponsors and other leaders must communicate powerfully and often, that this is not a Change Champions-alone effort. Culture change is about "We." As the new narratives emerge and spread, remind leaders to acknowledge people moving toward the TO state. And as HR and management systems are revised to align with emerging new narratives, leaders need to hold themselves and others accountable for using mindsets, language, and behaviors that reflect the new narratives.

Don't Overfocus on the Bright Spots

Sometimes there are pockets of success here and there across the organization, but the overall culture is mainly unchanged. If Change Champions focus only on these pockets of success, they can create bubbles—wonderful places of transformation talk that do not trigger systemic change (Schillinger, 2019).

To counter this tendency to overfocus on the bright spots, encourage Change Champions to keep "eyes and ears" on the state of readiness and the initial joining of groups in the effort to create and live a new narrative throughout the organization and to call out places where the new narrative seems to be moving slower. There might be a need for dialogue sessions and Executive Sponsor involvement. Ping surveys also provide good data about areas/functions/departments needing attention and improvement and where the organization needs to focus its attention to continue to build momentum for change.

Summary

Create structures to support the Change Champions during and after the formal education process. These support systems should be designed to help the Change Champion manage questions, challenges, and dilemmas and enable them to sustain their energy, focus, and commitment to the change effort and new narrative.

Checklist for Supporting Change Champions

- ✓ Encourage Change Champions to leverage all their sources of support during and after the formal education sessions.
- ✓ Engage Change Champions in dialogue to discuss common dilemmas and generate ideas for managing them in their education sessions, Pod meetings, and other working sessions.
- ✓ Suggest that some dilemmas are best handled by reframing and others by recontracting.
- ✓ Support Change Champions as they recontract with managers to maintain their support through the change process.
- ✓ Include managers in strategy and dialogue sessions so they see opportunities to benefit from and be part of the changes.
- ✓ Encourage Executive Sponsors to frequently communicate that this is a "We" effort and what leaders and others can do to avoid Change Champion burnout.

NINE

Our Wish for the Future

> Imagine getting diverse people to grapple with controversial economic and social issues. It would mean planning with a full spectrum of perspectives, including those impacted by the outcomes. This is a big step for many leaders who fear they will lose control and chaos will ensue. It takes faith that, at our core, our common humanity matters more than our differences. We are at a point when we must take a leap of faith into unknown territory. We no longer have a choice.
>
> —*Sandra Janoff,* Striving for Wholeness: It is Time for Social Scientists to Make a Big Noise

Leading change is not easy, and organizational system change is one of the most complex. The current cultural narratives in your organization might not be perfect or even good, but they are the storylines, mindsets, and behaviors most people have learned to navigate. The current narratives represent the current reality and changing them requires a total system change effort.

Leaders face a more significant challenge when creating a culture that values inclusion, equity, and access that leverages diversity. We live in a time of increased social polarization among groups of people regarding their economic or social circumstances and opportunities, their beliefs about people, and what kind of world, country, and organization we should have. People's fears and concerns move them to identify and feel most secure with those who share their beliefs. Therefore, organizational culture change feels personal to many people. You might be challenging some of their long-held beliefs about certain groups of people—"You are trying to change how I relate to other people." You might be challenging some personal preferences—"This is how I do things!"

"That is how my former manager did things!" "This is what makes this organization successful!"

We believe organizations of today and the future must unleash their people to enhance and transform *what is* to achieve their highest performance (OD Gathering, 2021). The stakes are high—almost win-lose. Organizations that underutilize team members' talents because of their cultural biases, limiting messages, or asking (directly or indirectly) for people to hide or make parts of themselves small are likely to lose the "war for talent" and not achieve their goals. They will probably lose the innovation that results from a diverse group of people mixing it up to create breakthroughs. And they will probably lose people's willingness to give their discretionary energy to improve the organization.

Organizations are perhaps the *one place* in our polarized society where people of diverse backgrounds and experiences work for a common purpose and shared success. This allows leaders to engage the organization's people in collective dialogue, disrupting narratives that no longer work for people and inviting the emergence of new narratives and images of the future. Sometimes the catalyst for a new narrative comes from a leader saying something that signals a change in expectations for the senior leadership team, as shown in this example:

> CEO Hal Yoh's organization faced complex market, technical, and government challenges as it sought to continue to grow its $3 billion family owned business. Hal understood that the organization needed to leverage its full range of skills, experience, and talent to manage these challenges and grow and prosper. And that began with the senior leaders. The business could only grow if leaders included, invested in, and engaged their people. They needed to hold themselves accountable for their own development as well.
>
> Hal framed the new expectations for all senior leaders as follows, a phrase which he repeated continually to the senior leaders: *"Grow your business, grow your people, grow yourself."* He emphasized that all three parts were equally important. The business flourished as leaders began demonstrating how they were growing people and themselves, and a new narrative about how the organization achieved its goals emerged.

The opportunity to be an even higher-performing organization with an enabling culture in which a diverse group of people can do their best work is right around the corner for many organizations. We can move from a culture of "I" to a new "We" that is even more high performing. Will you and your organization turn that corner, take that leap? If you have already, please write to us and tell us about your experience. If you haven't, share this book with your colleagues, have a dialogue about what can be, and start the journey to the new narratives that will allow your organization to thrive.

References

ASLA 2006 student awards. (2006). Retrieved from American Society of Landscape Architects: https://www.asla.org/awards/2006/studentawards/282.html

Baldwin, C. & Linnea, A. (2010). *The Circle Way: A leader in every chair.* Berrett-Koehler Publishers.

Barker, J. A. (1993). *Paradigms: The business of discovering the future.* Harper-Collins.

Block, P. (2018). *Community: The structure of belonging.* Berrett-Koehler Publishers.

Bratt, B. H. (2020). *The team discovered: Dialogic team coaching.* BMI Publishing.

Bushe, G. R. (2020). *The dynamics of generative change.* BMI Publishing.

Bushe, G. R. & Marshak, R. J. (2014). The dialogic mindset in organization development. *Research in organizational change and development* (pp. 55–97). Emerald.

Bushe, G. R. & Marshak, R. J. (2015). Introduction to the practice of dialogic OD. In G. R. Bushe & R. J. Marshak (Eds.), *Dialogic organization development: The theory and practice of transformational change* (pp. 33–56). Berrett-Koehler Publishers.

Bushe, G. R. & Storch, J. (2015). Generative image: Sourcing novelty. In G. R. Bushe, *Dialogic organization development: The theory and practice of transformational change* (pp. 101–122). Berrett-Koehler Publishers.

Cheung-Judge, M.-Y. (2001). The self as an instrument: A cornerstone for the future of OD. *OD Practitioner*, 33(3), 11–16.

Ellinor, L. & Gerard, G. (1998). *Dialogue: Rediscover the transforming power of conversation.* John Wiley & Sons, Inc.

Eoyang, G. & Holladay, R. J. (2013). *Adaptive action: Leveraging uncertainty in your organization.* Stanford University Press.

Ferdman, B.M. (2010). Teaching inclusion by example and experience: Creating an inclusive learning environment. In K. M. Hannum, *Leading across differences: Cases and perspectives—Facilitator's guide* (pp. 37–50). Pfeiffer.

Ferdman, B. M. (2017). Paradoxes of inclusion: Understanding and managing the tensions of diversity and multiculturalism. *Journal of Applied Behavioral Science,* 53 (2), 235–263. https://doi.org/10.1177/0021886317702608

Heifetz, R. & Linsky, M. (2017). *Leadership on the line: Staying alive through the dangers of change.* Harvard Business Review Press.

Holman, P. (2010). *Engaging emergence: Turning upheaval into opportunity.* Berrett-Koehler Publishers.

Janoff, S. (2021). Striving for wholeness: It is time for social scientists to make a big noise. In J. M. Bartunek, *Social scientists confronting global crisis* (pp. 22–28). Routledge.

Jensen, M. & Miller, F. A. (1995, 1997, 2022). *Learning community behaviors: A safe place/zone.* The Kaleel Jamison Consulting Group, Inc.
Katz, J. H. & Miller, F. A. (2010). Inclusion: The HOW for the next organizational breakthrough. In W. J. Rothwell, J. M. Stavros, R. L. Sullivan, and A. Sullivan (Eds.), *Practicing organization development: A guide for leading change* (3rd ed. pp.436–445) John Wiley and Sons.
Katz, J. H. & Miller, F. A. (2013). *Opening doors to teamwork and collaboration: 4 keys that change EVERYTHING.* Berrett-Koehler Publishers.
Kluckhohn, C., Murray, H. A., & Schneider, D. M. (Eds.). (1953). *Personality in nature, society, and culture* (2nd ed.). Knopf.
Marshak, R. J. & Heracleous, L. (2022). The effect of evocative frames on strategic decisions. *The Journal of Applied Behavioral Science*, Advance online publication. https://doi.org/10.1177%2F00218863221104864
McKergow, M. (2021). *Hosting generative change: Creating containers for creativity and commitment.* BMI Publishing.
Miller, F. A. & Davis-Howard, V. (2022). It's time for organizations to take a leap forward. *The Organization Development Journal,* 40(1), 43–62.
Miller, F. A. & Katz, J. H. (2002). *The inclusion breakthrough: Unleashing the real power of diversity.* Berrett-Koehler Publishers.
Miller, F. A. & Katz, J. H. (2005). Inclusion starts with "hello". In M. Silberman (Ed.), *The ASTD Team & Organization Development Sourcebook* (pp. 5–8). American Society for Training & Development.
Miller, F. A. & Katz, J. H. (2018). *Safe enough to soar.* Berrett-Koehler Publishers.
Minahan, M. & Forrester, R. (2020). Exactly how do you use yourself? *Organization Development Review*, 52 (1), 8–16.
National Association of Colleges & Employers. (2021). *NACE's diversity, equity, and inclusion statement.* Retrieved from Naceweb.org: https://www.naceweb.org/about-us/equity-definition/
OD Gathering. (2021). *Moving the OD field forward.* Unpublished manuscript. https://drive.google.com/file/d/1rKD_2_vxRfQJmaMC-E4FXpUXOaLbTf6Y/view
Roehrig, M. J., Schwendenwein, J., & Bushe, G. R. (2015). Amplifying change: A three-phase approach to model, nurture, and embed ideas for change. In G. R. Bushe & R. J. Marshak (Eds.), *Dialogic organization development: The theory and practice of transformational change* (pp. 325–348). Berrett-Koehler Publishers.
Schein, E. H. & Schein, P.A. (2019). *The corporate culture survival guide.* (3rd edition). Wiley.
Schillinger, C. (2019, January 7). *Culture and the real impact of change agents-part 2.* Retrieved from weneedsocial.com: http://weneedsocial.com/blog/2019/1/1/culture-and-the-real-impact-or-change-agents
Senge, P. M. (1990). *The fifth discipline: The art & practice of the learning organization.* Doubleday.

Senge, P. M., Kleiner, A., Roberts, C., Ross, R. B., & Smith, B. J. (1994). *The fifth discipline fieldbook: Strategies and tools for building a learning organization.* Doubleday.

Shepard, H. A. (1975). Rules of thumb for change agents. *Organization development practitioner*, 1–5.

Southern, N. (2015). Framing inquiry: The art of engaging great questions. In G. R. Bushe & R. J. Marshak (Eds.), *Dialogic organization development: The theory and practice of transformational change* (pp. 269-289). Berrett-Koehler Publishers.

Stacey, R. (1996). *Complexity and creativity in organizations.* Berrett-Koehler Publishers.

Stacey, R. (2015). Understanding organizations as complex responsive processes of relating. In G. R. Bushe & R. J. Marshak (Eds.), *Dialogic organization development: The theory and practice of transformational change* (pp. 151–175). Berrett-Koehler Publishers.

Stirling-Wilke, G. (2021). *From physical place to virtual space: How to design and host transformative spaces online.* BMI Publishing.

Swart, C. (2015). Coaching from a dialogic OD paradigm. In G. R. Bushe & R. J. Marshak (Eds.), *Dialogic organization development: The theory and practice of transformational change* (pp. 349–370). Berrett-Koehler Publishers.

Waldman, D. A. & Sparr, J. L. (2022). Rethinking Diversity Strategies: An Application of Paradox and Positive Organization Behavior Theories. *Academy of Management Perspectives.* Advance online publication. https://doi.org/10.5465/amp.2021.0183

Wasserman, I. C. (2015, June 29). Dialogic OD, diversity and inclusion: Aligning mindsets, values, and practices. *Research in organizational change and development*, 329–356.

Watkins, K. E. & Marsick, V. J. (1993). *Sculpting the learning organization: Lessons in the art and science of systemic change.* Jossey-Bass Inc.

Wenger, E. C. (1998). *Communities of practice: Learning, meaning, and identity.* Cambridge University Press.

Wheatley, M. (2007). *Finding Our Way.* Berrett-Koehler Publishers.

The Kaleel Jamison Consulting Group, Inc. was founded in 1970 by Kaleel Jamison (1931–1985). It is the oldest Organization Development (OD) firm and the oldest firm that has a core competency in inclusion, leveraging diversity and culture change. In 1993, KJCG coined the use of inclusion as a core concept for organization cultures.

Made in the USA
Middletown, DE
30 November 2022